Remote Work for MILITARY SPOUSES

Find and Grow Your Meaningful Mobile Career

Laura Briggs

Elva Resa ∗ Saint Paul

Library of Congress Control Number: 2022936499

ISBNs 978-1-934617-65-6 (pb), 978-1-934617-75-5 (epub)

1L 2 3 4 5

Elva Resa Publishing
8362 Tamarack Vlg, Ste 119-106
St Paul, MN 55125

ElvaResa.com
MilitaryFamilyBooks.com

To John,
for always supporting my career and dreams

Contents

Introduction

I spent eight years working toward a career in education, earning a master's degree in political science, and working on my PhD in public administration and policy at night while I taught during the day as a middle school geography teacher. Then, I submitted my resignation.

My decision was a hard one to make. I was walking away from years of training. I had planned to become a tenure-track professor at a university. But that career choice did not mesh well with the Navy's plans for my then-boyfriend's future. So I chose to pivot my career and start fresh when my now-husband got his next set of military orders.

I started by searching online: "How to become a freelance writer." In the years that followed—including the nine moves we tackled together—I adapted my career into a fully remote mix of working as a home-based freelancer and a full-time remote marketing director. Working remotely empowered me to take my work anywhere and not let my career take a backseat just because my spouse was an active-duty service member.

While there were plenty of road bumps, rejections, mistakes, and career issues to navigate during that period, there were also incredible rewards, such as a bigger professional network, more opportunities to learn new things, and being considered for positions I'd never thought of before.

This snapshot of my experience is just one of hundreds of thousands of stories from military spouses who have had to pause, pivot, give up on, or otherwise change their career plans because they married into the military. While each journey is unique, there are common threads. I wrote this book because of the common challenges military spouses face. Being a military spouse does not mean you aren't deserving of a meaningful career. I want to help you find a career that moves with you when those orders inevitably come.

Why did you pick up this book? Did you seek it out intentionally or was it given to you by a friend or an organization helping you with your job search for remote employment? Knowing why you picked up this book is just as important as the contents. The first step to remote success is understanding why it interests you in the first place.

No matter how you landed here, this book is designed to give you the tools to make decisions about remote work: if it's right for you, how you want to work remotely, what work-life balance looks like for you, and more. If you've decided that remote work is indeed a fit for you, you'll uncover information in these pages about how to find jobs, apply for them, stand out in interviews, and even negotiate your employment offer. If you decide remote work is not a good fit, that's valuable to know too!

There is a lot of promise in the possibilities of remote work options, but it is not always an easy journey. It might take a month to find the perfect position or you may feel stuck in application mode for a few months, filling out endless forms in hopes of an interview. A final interview you nailed may end with an offer going to another candidate. Perhaps the hardest of these challenges is the waiting, since it can take a long time to get interest from a company and to move forward with the hiring process.

Stick with it. Your military lifestyle has prepared you to be resilient, adaptable, and savvy. If you want this, you will make it work, and these resources will help you get there.

Chapter 1 —

Why Remote, Why Now?

The world of employment has changed significantly in recent years, largely due to advances in technology. Those advances have prompted many employers to rethink their work arrangements: Is it really necessary for everyone to be in a physical office every day to perform well?

Some employers choose to have a completely in-office workforce or multiple locations where all employees report to a physical place of work. Others choose to have a fully-remote or distributed workforce. Many land somewhere in the middle with hybrid teams.

With the impacts of the global COVID-19 pandemic, employers have been forced to realize the possibilities of remote work. Many had to pivot their teams to work remotely for an extended period of time during the pandemic, which meant they had to adapt their communication culture, technology, and overall strategies to be successful. However, even without the push of a global pandemic, many companies were already transitioning to a hybrid work environment, leveraging remote employees or independent contractors to get projects done. In general, this is good news for most military spouses.

Military spouses who decide they are the right fit for remote employment are empowered to develop meaningful careers that stay with them from one base to another. Not every military spouse will be the right fit for remote work, but if you've picked up this book, there's a good chance you believe you have the skills to succeed in a digital environment.

For many military spouses, it is difficult to take the time to focus on their own career when there are so many other ways to spend precious time and energy. You may wonder *"Is this the right time to try to make this transition? What if our orders change? What if there are unexpected shifts in family or school life?"* While these might seem like barriers to a career shift, they are also the perfect reasons to shift to a remote career path. If you have the drive—which you will decide—and the skills and resources—which you will learn in the following chapters—then now is the perfect time to leverage your need for a location-independent career as a military spouse.

Know that each company determines how remote work contributes to its culture and meets its needs. As a remote job seeker, understanding the different options and styles of remote work can help you determine the types of industries or companies to engage.

Landscape of Military Spouse Unemployment

One of the biggest challenges military spouses face is the ability to obtain and maintain meaningful career options. It can be difficult to secure positions that accommodate career progression in a mobile lifestyle.

Despite significant investment by the US Department of Defense (DoD) to address this issue and leverage nonprofit network support, about a quarter of military spouses are unemployed and more than half report underemployment, in which their qualifications and skills far exceed job requirements. Even in underemployment situations, the military lifestyle can make it hard for spouses to find and hold a position.

Under- and unemployment can cause a flurry of negative impacts on the quality of life for military spouses and families. These include frustration in marriages and significant relationships because the non-military partner is unable to pursue their professional goals, a lack of financial security for the entire family, negative feelings toward the military for the non-military partner, and even negative feelings about whether or not a service member should stay in the military.

These issues become most impactful when a service couple reaches mid-career and peak earning potential years. Retaining service members is a significant priority for national security and staffing purposes, which is why DoD and other organizations have made military spouse unemployment a top priority.

Working is not always about financial security, although it can be a driving factor. Military spouses also want to earn educational and professional achievements. Many feel they have to take a step back—or multiple steps back—in their career over the course of their marriage to a service member. This can be frustrating and overwhelming, especially when a spouse may have just enough time to get used to a particular base location and their new position before having to change and start all over again.

Furthermore, military spouses often have unique needs when it comes to flexibility and lifestyle. They need to be able to support their family and provide childcare, especially in the case of military trainings and deployments, which impact their day-to-day life on short notice. Since spouses often have to pivot and adapt, remote work has become an even more important consideration for military families.

Make Room for Your Career

Military spouses face unique challenges in developing their careers, because, in most cases, their service member's career comes first. Some spouses may feel happy—empowered even—as a stay-at-home parent, allowing them to support their service member's career, raise their family, and manage household duties. However, others are determined to maintain their individual career identity. For those military spouses who want to work, remote work can be a great option. Working remotely offers employees the opportunity to accomplish more, eliminate commute times, reduce their stress levels, save money, and bring their career with them no matter where they live.

While these benefits are appealing, wanting a remote position and being able to thrive in a remote position are different things. Understanding what a remote position requires will force you to think more carefully about the natural skill sets and personality traits you bring to the table and to understand where you may need to hone your skills.

Taking the time to identify your natural and learned skills and to analyze what you want most out of your remote career will make your journey infinitely more rewarding. Military spouses already deal with obstacles that average job seekers don't—like resume gaps due to moving—so the practice of removing the guesswork surrounding what you want to do and what you are good at from your job hunt will help your career journey develop a bit smoother from the beginning. I'll discuss more about self-evaluation and job-evaluation in later chapters.

Employers and Remote Work

Did you know that not all remote jobs allow you to work completely from home? In fact, the majority of remote jobs are actually a combination of at-home and in-office work. With at-home work, you'll want to read between the lines on any job descriptions to determine the level of remote work that is being offered with that company. It is critical to know if any type of location requirement is listed in the job description, as this will mean needing to live within that local area or traveling to that area on a regular basis, which might not be possible for military spouses.

Why a Remote Job May Require In-Person Work

There are many different reasons why employers offering at-home jobs could still require certain geographic locations. These include:

▷ Trainings or meetings in which the company needs onsite or ongoing training to take place in-person.

▷ Clients. Remote workers may need to interface directly with clients for in-person meetings, troubleshooting, physical assessments, or sales calls.

▷ Travel. Positions that require a significant amount of travel may need to be placed near a company's main office or a specific airport to make travel more efficient or cost effective.

▷ Taxes and insurance. Companies are registered to pay and collect taxes or provide employment-related insurance in certain locations. Registering in a new location for one remote employee can create a significant administrative burden, so some job descriptions will have specific US state residency requirements.

▷ Legal reasons, such as government regulations, licensing requirements, or professional licensing certifications that require a person to perform duties on-site, in person, or within a certain locale.

▷ Collaboration, equipment, or access to sensitive data. The nature of the work may require use of a laboratory, access to physical equipment or a manufacturing plant, or high levels of security not achievable in remote locations.

Terms Employers Use in Relation to Remote Work

▷ A "work-from-anywhere" job refers to remote employment that can be done from home, no matter where you live. There are no location requirements for a work-from-anywhere position.

▷ A "telecommuting option" job allows for some occasional at-home work, and you'll want to read the specifics of the job description and discuss this with the hiring manager so that you are clear about how often you'll be allowed to work at home with some telecommuting available. There is usually a mix of at-home and on-site work.

▷ A "mostly telecommuting" role requires occasional on-site work with the vast majority of the work being done from home.

▷ A "100 percent telecommute" job can be done entirely from your home but might still have location requirements.

Licensing Considerations

Many spouses work in fields that require state certifications or licenses such as education, cosmetology, legal, and healthcare, among others. While some of these are in-person jobs, the volume of remote careers in fields like healthcare and education is on the rise. The specifics of what's required for each will vary from one state to another and from one field to another. One of the most important things to keep in mind is the importance of doing research in advance to create an appropriate timeline so you know what to expect.

Here are some ways to make sure you're prepared for potential licensing considerations:

▷ Create a binder with information about potential duty stations, if known. Research each of those states and their specific requirements.

▷ Keep a binder and folder of all your primary documents associated with your career, such as copies of your degree and current state licenses as well as your CV and employment history for easy reference.

▷ Call credentialing organizations directly to ask if they have reciprocity arrangements in place. Some industries and states will accept your credentials from your current state.

▷ Gather information in advance while you're still in contact with those in your current role. For example, if you need a letter of recommendation from a principal, supervising therapist, or other employer, ask them for this in advance even if it's a template in which they can add specific details later. Prepare your contacts to hear from specific state boards or commissions so they're not caught off guard when contacted for employment verification or a reference.

▷ Determine how long the average approval takes for someone requesting a new license or training.

As soon as you know where you will move, begin submitting materials or preparing. Some states might require exams, fees, or additional education for you to be certified in your new location.

▷ Seek out networking groups. Ask other spouses about their experiences and find out other issues to be aware of as you start this process. Many groups advocate on behalf of military spouses or support specific career requirements. For example, the Military Spouse JD Network is an excellent source for attorneys moving to a new state, particularly if your move would require taking that state's bar exam in addition to meeting other lawyer licensing requirements.

▷ Check with your service branch or Military Community and Family Policy programs. In many cases, you might be able to get reimbursed for the costs of a new license under the National Defense Authorization Act.

Common Remote Jobs

If you are not already in a chosen career, you may want to research which industries or job fields interest you that more frequently or easily adapt to remote work, such as:

▷ Data entry

▷ Sales

▷ Computers and information technology (IT)

▷ Writing and editing

▷ Account management

▷ Marketing

▷ Medical transcription, triage, and administration

▷ Customer service

▷ Engineering

▷ Operations

▷ Business development

▷ Accounting and finance

▷ Software development

▷ Project management

▷ Human resources and recruiting

Within each of these industries you're likely to find a mix of everything on the spectrum, from in-person positions to fully remote. Research to determine if any of these are the best fit for you and make sure your interests line up with individual job descriptions.

Remote work can make career continuity in military life easier, but there are plenty of other reasons why it makes sense.

Benefits of Remote Work

When structured properly and with consideration of any unique aspects of the company, remote work can have far-reaching benefits for both employers and employees.

For Employers

For a long time, remote work was looked at as an unusual way of maintaining a career, mostly used by freelancers, artists, and other independent professionals. Allowing team members to telecommute even one day per week was an uncommon perk welcomed by employees who needed it.

Today, far fewer employers have to be convinced that remote work, in some capacity, is a viable option. Benefits include cost savings, expanded talent pools, reductions in missed work, increased productivity, and loyalty. Technology improvements offer more possibilities than ever before.

Cost Savings

When employers leverage a remote workforce, they can decrease physical office location expenses. Even for those that leverage part-time telecommuting, desk sharing enables the company to reduce the size of its overall office. This can also reduce expenses for furniture, cleaning equipment, building maintenance, utilities, and more.

Expanded Talent Pools

Previously, employers were limited by the number of applicants in a specific geographic area. By offering remote work, companies can expand the talent pool. Employers now have access to the most qualified employees regardless of their location. This makes it easier to leverage staff with specialized skills and reduces the time and expenses for training. Furthermore, there are no relocation costs for remote workers, which could save thousands of dollars depending on the industry.

Reductions in Missed Work

For the most part, if a remote employee feels slightly sick, they are more likely to continue working than their physical-location counterparts. They don't have to travel or drive into the office and can take extra rest breaks if needed. An on-site employee with a long commute or contagious symptoms is more likely to call in sick. (Remote workers should take sick time off when needed.) The same goes for time taken off for events or appointments. If the employer is flexible, a remote employee can structure their day around their work and won't have to take unnecessary time off.

Increased Productivity

With modern technology, internet, and communication tools, team members can keep in touch easily without feeling tethered to a desk. This can promote positive feelings of motivation and productivity, which may mean the difference between employees who want to go the extra mile and those who just want to make it through the workday.

This engagement is a win-win for employers and employees because employees will use their time more productively as they work from home. This can significantly increase a company's bottom line when it's leveraged across all the departments in which it makes sense to go remote. With increased productivity, companies can focus on growth and tackling new challenges, putting them at the forefront of innovation. With the fast pace of change and competitive markets, companies that function well and innovatively are poised to grow faster.

Loyalty

Employees who work for a company or organization that aligns with their personal values and who feel trusted to do their job even when not in a physical office, have a greater sense of loyalty toward their employer. If happy employees desire or need to move, they can do so without having to weigh the option of leaving their company. Higher levels of freedom and flexibility also increase job satisfaction. By increasing employee retention, employers save the cost of hiring and training a new employee and reduce the disruption to existing teams.

Technology Enables Remote Work

Today's technology allows employers in a variety of industries to perform well without an in-office workforce. Digital platforms, video conferencing, online project management tools, messaging apps, and other technology options enable effective communication and collaboration from remote offices.

Lightweight, fast computers and the prevalence of easily downloadable software may reduce the need for a centralized IT infrastructure. Reliance on remote technology also forces a company to adapt and grow technology solutions out of necessity. Proactive technology adoption strategies can give companies a competitive edge throughout their business.

For Employees

Employees reap benefits from working from the comfort of their homes, too. When it's the right fit for the company and for the individual worker's style, benefits can include cost and time savings, more flexibility and freedom, location independence, better focus, improved health and wellness, and the possibility of better work-life balance.

Cost Savings

The costs of commuting, professional work attire, eating out, and parking are some of the most common expenses associated with working in an office. Remote work can reduce these expenses significantly. If you are a working parent, you may have additional options for childcare in or near your home that may reduce those costs as well.

Time Savings

Without a commute, remote workers easily add time into their daily routines. For military spouses, this may be even more detectable in the time saved searching for and settling into a new job after each move.

Flexibility and Freedom

Many remote employees are able to manage their own schedules, even when they have set working hours. When you have clarity with your employer about the hours that you must work or be available, you can structure your work more easily around the military lifestyle.

Location Independence

When employees are not bound to the company's physical buildings, they are free to move or travel when it suits them. Remote work enables military spouses to keep their jobs and minimize the impacts of transitional periods.

Higher Levels of Focus

At an in-person office, employees have less control over noise, discomfort, disruptions, and other distractions that increase the stopping and restarting of work or that make their work environment less productive. A remote employee who understands how they work best can create that work environment at home. Both employee and employer reap the benefits of greater levels of focus.

Better Health and Overall Happiness

Remote workers face no risk of getting sick from the office environment and can also find mental health benefits, like decreased stress. Happier employees translates into increased productivity and better work quality.

Better Work-Life Balance

When structured properly, the ability to work remotely gives employees more control in their lives, allowing for better balance between personal and professional endeavors. They can decrease engagement in office politics, take breaks when needed, and limit distractions. They don't have to transport laptops, files, or other equipment back and forth, so they can spend less time reorganizing their workspace at the start or end of the day. They aren't rushing to catch a commuter train or sitting in traffic. This translates to less stress and more time to spend with loved ones or pursuing personal interests.

If you picked up this book, there's a good chance you were already sold on all the benefits of working remotely. But if you can put yourself in your current or prospective employer's position, you'll be set up much more effectively to help them understand why remote work makes sense. This is essential if you are already in a job that you are happy with and you want to convince your employer to take your role remote.

Many military spouses are familiar with this scenario: You worked hard to get into your position and have thrived as an in-office employee, but now you've received Permanent Change of Station (PCS) orders. Or perhaps you and your partner agreed to live separately while your career got off the ground, but now you both want to live together, meaning that you'll need to move. If you'd like to keep your current job or avoid the extensive remote job hunt, consider whether or not your current employer might let you work remotely.

Convince Your Current Employer

One often under-explored option for military spouses who have already built up credibility, trust, and experience with a current employer is to suggest a remote work proposal. This is most applicable when there are no existing telecommuting policies in place.

Your employer surely recognizes that there are significant costs to losing you as an employee, both in terms of the replacement cost of finding someone else and the downtime while that new person trains for a role. Before asking your supervisor outright if they would be open to you working remotely, consider putting together a comprehensive telecommuting proposal that shows you have put great thought and care into making this recommendation. Showing that you have done your research is one of the best things you can do when attempting to convince someone else that this is a good fit for both you and the company.

This proposal should express the points of concern that may come up for your employer and should show that you have thought about how your job may need to be adapted to a remote work environment. A cover letter can be helpful for explaining the overall situation and your recommendations, especially if multiple people on your current team will need to review this proposal.

Craft Your Remote Work Proposal

An introduction will tell your supervisor what you're asking for and why it has positive benefits for the company. You will be able to expand on your points later. Keep this short and sweet in the beginning of the proposal, and remember to provide any background information that reminds the employer about why they're happy to work with you. This can include previous employment reviews, special achievements or awards you earned, and other qualifications. If there are other people who are currently leveraging telecommuting or flexible work policies, bring this up as well. Keep this section to a couple of paragraphs.

In the next section of your proposal, describe how this arrangement would look for you. This includes things like hours, technology, job tasks, communication, accountability, costs, and logistics. You will need to think about who will be responsible for handling any adaptations, such as technology that might be needed. Remember that this is really about the technology and communication required for this arrangement to work, which means thinking not just about your individual role but also the ways you collaborate and work with other members of the team.

In the third part of your proposal, address the benefits the company would enjoy that are specific to your role. Will telecommuting help you do your job more effectively and with more focus? Although you certainly are making a proposal that working from home is necessary for your personal life, don't lead with this. Remember that focusing on your ability to do your job and the overall benefits for the company can be much more convincing. While you want to keep as much of the proposal as positive as possible, don't overlook potential problems and solutions. Presenting potential issues clearly and offering potential solutions will show that you've given the arrangement real thought.

If there really are obvious standout problems, then you must think about possible solutions for addressing these. This will also help you navigate the conversation you'll have with your supervisor after submitting your proposal. Examples of common challenges that might come up would be childcare or different time zones. State your suggestions. At the conclusion of your proposal, give your supervisor a next recommended step, such as welcoming an in-depth discussion.

Not every position will work well remotely, and not every company will be open to this proposal. But such a proposal may help you stay in a position you enjoy, while avoiding periods of unemployment and yet another job search. And it may prove beneficial for your employer as well—helping the company avoid hiring and training expenses and a temporary decrease of productivity.

If you are able to convince your current employer to let you go remote, the rest of this book will be helpful as you learn more about the challenges and successes of working remotely and what employers need to see for such a proposal to work long term.

If convincing your current employer to go remote does not work, rest assured there are plenty of remote opportunities in many different industries that will allow you to obtain and grow a meaningful career while supporting your partner's unique military lifestyle.

Chapter 2 —

Evaluate Your Options

D eciding how to pursue a career, business, or other opportunity as a military spouse is a highly personal exercise. This chapter is designed to present you with an overview of the remote work options available to military spouses, help you define why you are seeking remote work, and introduce you to the tools you'll need to succeed at it.

When you first seek out a remote employment position, it's about more than finding a job you're qualified for that allows you to work from any location or time zone. It's about making sure that remote work aligns with your personal and professional goals and that you're properly set up to succeed in a remote work environment. There is no one size fits all when it comes to work and careers for military spouses. There are many options available.

Employment Status

Remote work fits into a variety of temporary, seasonal, and permanent positions as well as part-time or full-time statuses. Consider the best employment status for you now as well as where you want to be in your next position.

No Active Employment

There are numerous reasons why a military spouse might feel that no active employment is the right fit for their family at any given time. Perhaps they're in another country and their spouse is working long hours, constantly training, or deployed, so the best current option is to work as the primary caregiver in the home. Perhaps after stepping out of the workforce, it's time to recalibrate before pursuing a different job or career.

Volunteering

Many spouses volunteer as a way to build community, give back, and continue to develop their skills. Volunteering is an excellent way to remain active in work-type projects without the commitment that paid work brings. It can also be a great way to build a bridge back into the workforce after time away.

Part-Time Employment

More flexible than full-time employment but possibly with some of the same benefits, part-time employment allows workers the stability of working with the same company without having to commit to a full work week. This can free up hours for other pursuits, like parenting, caregiving, volunteering, learning, training, or working on contract projects.

Full-Time Employment

Full-time employment with an established company offers a sense of stability and a regular paycheck. It may provide continuity for advancement opportunities, help you stay current in a specific career field, or may be necessary for managerial responsibilities. Full-time remote employment is also a great option for people who want the flexibility and control of remote work, but don't want to take on the pressure or potential risk of running their own business.

Self-Employment

Owning a business or working independently for one or multiple companies is a common choice for military spouses. Whether a business is client- or product-based, there are logistical and legal challenges to moving a business, but military spouses can set up their businesses to be mobile friendly.

Freelance or independent contractor work offers the flexibility to accept or decline assignments as needed, but requires active management of opportunities and is another form of owning a business. Jobs may be paid on an hourly, project, or retainer basis. Federal and state regulations define independent contractor status as well as estimated taxes and other self-employment requirements.

Although this is a viable way to earn income remotely as a military spouse, and a great way to supplement income in general, this book will focus on employment-based careers with companies other than your own.

Working remotely has transitioned from being a luxury for a select few or an option a few days a week, into a priority for some companies and a necessity for others in light of the COVID-19 pandemic. Increasingly, employers are open to the idea of using remote workers either exclusively or as a part of their hybrid team. At the same time, more employees and contractors are looking for the option to work remotely.

Many companies have an increasing interest in partnering with military spouses and veteran-affiliated career professionals as part of their overall mission of giving back. While there are certainly plenty of reasons that you might be looking for a job specifically because it has remote flexibility, you need to make sure that you understand the other reasons why you are the right fit for a particular remote position or employer.

This comes down to knowing your "why."

Define Your Reasons for Remote Work

Your "why" is crucial for defining the direction of your future career search. It will help you identify job opportunities that are most in line with your individual needs and goals, and properly position yourself to those employers. This will help drive you to the right remote opportunities.

Imagine, for example, that you need extreme flexibility in your schedule. When you open a job post and it clearly lists that you need to be available at set times every single day, it will be easy for you to realize that this does not align with your specific needs. If your reason for working remotely is flexibility for your family, only consider remote jobs that meet your underlying scheduling requirements.

There is a good chance that most of the reasons supporting your desire to work remotely are personal to you. A few common motivations include wanting to:

> ▷ Be in the workforce, especially if you were an active career professional prior to military life.

> ▷ Push yourself professionally or maintain opportunities for advancement.

> ▷ Be part of a team contributing toward a greater mission and goal.

> ▷ Learn new skills that can develop you personally and as a professional.

> ▷ Earn additional income to support your family.

> ▷ Be a good role model for your children and other family members.

▷ Give back to organizations and people you care about.

▷ Feel motivated to wake up each day to work on projects or with team members that excite you.

All of these reasons might be specific to you, and some might not apply at all. This concept of having a "why" will be woven throughout your job search, including in cover letters, interviews, and even throughout your resume. Knowing these motivations before you apply will help you communicate your needs and goals at various stages of the application process.

Of course, a substantial part of the reason you want to work remotely is the ability to have your job follow you when you move. Many military spouses are led to believe that their military affiliation is a negative for their career prospects, but you can spin this as a win for the employer. Given that more employers than ever are open to having a conversation around remote work, you can bring this up as one of the reasons you are seeking remote employment—to identify a long-term opportunity where you can succeed and grow with a company while limiting the impact of your mobility as a military spouse.

Remote work certainly is not without its challenges, but the best way you can identify this proposition for an employer is to be prepared to talk about why this not only benefits you, but also benefits the company as well. Consider options such as not having to pay for office space, getting to partner with the best talent regardless of location, and getting employees who might be more engaged and less stressed overall.

Showcase Your "Why"

Your reasons why you want to work remotely will come up regularly and can be used to help answer difficult questions in interviews, such as how you would handle being in different time zones or the challenges associated with communicating with a team primarily through email, video calls, and messaging systems.

Knowing your remote work goals adds a personal layer to the applications and interviews you have with potential employers. A desire to work remotely simply is not enough to differentiate you from dozens or even hundreds of other candidates. If it's a remote position, everyone else who applied wants to work remotely too. If it's not, there's still a good chance others will pitch the company the same way you will. Instead, you can showcase the skills you have that help remote workers succeed, showing the hiring team that you already have an understanding of what is necessary, even if you've never worked remotely before.

For example, you can lean into the facts that you're highly adaptable, familiar with technology, and have a quiet and consistent home working space. Use examples from previous positions to show your technology knowledge and adaptability. When an employer asks a question about the challenges of remote work in an interview, you can bring the conversation back to your motivation to be in that particular career field. In that instance, you have the opportunity to talk about what your career in that industry means to you, and the challenges you have faced while serving as a military spouse and putting your partner's career first.

What You Need to Work Remotely

Aside from the drive and passion to be successful with a remote opportunity, there are some specific items that should be lined up in order for you to be successful. This shows an employer that you have already done the necessary legwork to recognize how to be most effective with an at-home office as part of a remote team.

An Area to Work

First of all, one of the most important things you can have already set up before you even begin the application and interview process is a place to work. This does not need to be a room in and of itself, but it should be a quiet place with a closed door if possible.

You might need to reconfigure a closet or a utility room into a home office if you don't have the square footage in your apartment or home to make things work. You should also have a comfortable office chair and a sturdy desk surface. This can be a table or a countertop or even a shelf built into a wall as a standing desk. The point is that it should be one stationary place from which you can work remotely. This makes it easier to mentally check in and out of work on a daily basis, and it also presents a powerful front to the employers you are speaking with that you already have a dedicated space where you will report to work each day.

Having a professional-looking workspace with a closed door shows that you have thought about possible distractions and ways to remain focused on the job. As you are thinking about which room or section of your home you could potentially repurpose into your office, consider the background as well. You don't want huge windows behind your desk because these can cast light during the day and make it difficult for people to see you on video.

Ideally you'll want a calm, clean background, so avoid setting up a home office area with the kids' playroom in the background or with your bed or area you use to fold laundry. Any time you're on a meeting or a video call, anyone who sees your background should recognize that this is professional and clean looking. Filters and virtual backgrounds may work for temporary situations, but should not be your everyday solution.

Technology to Get the Job Done

Of course, you'll need to have the right technology in order to be successful in your at-home office. At a minimum this includes a computer or laptop and a high-speed internet connection. Depending on your intended job, you might need additional equipment as well.

It's a good idea to have a headset or earbuds available so you don't get feedback on video calls. Most employers are going to expect this as a bare minimum, so don't wait to purchase earbuds until after you've scheduled an interview. Have your office fully set up to be as functional as possible from the moment you begin applying.

A Plan for Minimizing Distractions

As you are thinking about what you really need to work remotely, consider how your location and work schedule can best minimize distractions.

For parents of school-age children, it can be a challenge to manage at-home work when school schedules unexpectedly change. Due to the pandemic, most districts now have virtual learning technology in place at least part of the time. Some schools have changed procedures to allow what used to be lost-learning days, such as snow days, to become online learning days. This means instead of a day of play with a caregiver, students may need to be on a computer attending class. You will need a backup plan for those virtual learning days, as well as days your child is home sick, or when other family members are home during your work hours

Setting boundaries and having discussions with family members is important. For example, when your door is closed and a particular hanger like "do not disturb" is outside the door, family members should know they cannot knock, run by screaming, or throw open the door, because you are likely in the middle of a meeting.

It's a good idea to have these conversations well in advance because this is a popular interview question that comes up around remote work. Everyone is going to have distractions and interruptions sometimes, but doing your due diligence to show that you've thought about this and have been proactive in setting up your home office and preparing your family for your remote work goes a long way with employers. They may also ask about your pets. Your cat walking across your keyboard during a video call may seem cute to you, but an employer may see it as you not maintaining a focused work environment.

An Extra Focus on Communication Skills

You will need excellent communication skills to work remotely. While this isn't a tangible item like a desk or the right computer with a high-speed internet connection, it is perhaps even more important. When you don't have the benefit of being with people in the same room, you need to work harder to infer meaning and reduce misunderstandings.

Instant messages and email can easily be misinterpreted, and it's not always possible to read someone's body language when you only see them from the chest up on a video call. Prepare for how you will connect with others effectively, and how you will handle challenges and miscommunications in a remote work environment. Be prepared with examples to demonstrate to a potential employer that you are a proactive, clear communicator.

Employee Versus Contractor

There are a few different ways to work remotely, but when reviewing job postings, the most important distinction to be mindful of is the one between employee and contractor.

The US Internal Revenue Service (IRS) provides guidelines that can help you understand whether being an employee or a contractor is the right fit for you. The IRS looks at issues of behavioral control, financial control, and relationship when making a decision over whether or not a position should be classified as an employee or contractor relationship.

For behavioral control, a worker is an employee when the company directs when and how the work is done. Financial control indicators include method of payment, opportunity for profit or loss in the company, and if the employer invests in equipment. Benefits, relationship permanency, and any contracts that detail the relationship can help to determine if someone is an employee versus a contractor.

Understanding an Employee Role

Most workers are familiar with an employee role. Employees are paid on a salaried or hourly basis and the employer is responsible for providing the necessary tools for you to do your job. In more traditional employment scenarios, an employer also provides the physical location where you work. The work is determined by the employer and delivered during hours the employer chooses. The employer deducts necessary taxes from your wages and at the end of the year sends employees a W-2 wage statement summarizing pay and deductions.

Depending on its size, the employer might also provide other benefits, such as health insurance, paid time off, stipends, supplements for technology, and even profit sharing.

A key determining factor of being an employee is that the company determines when and how you do the work. They determine the specifics of your job description. The intention is that you will remain in the employment scenario until either party decides to terminate that working relationship. In other words, this is often not intended to be a short-term working relationship, but rather a long-term partnership between the employee and the employer. These factors are important when distinguishing between employee and contractor status.

Understanding a Contractor Role

Contractors are typically paid a set per-project or hourly rate agreed upon between the contractor and client. In most cases, contractors work on a short-term basis, but it is not uncommon for some companies to use contractors on a long-term basis for as-needed or part-time work.

Many companies hire contractors because it allows them to create teams with specific skills for defined projects, rather than pay salary and benefits for an employee who may not have all the skills needed for a wide range of projects.

As a contractor, you are responsible for paying your own taxes, including any required estimated tax payments. Contractors do not receive the same benefits, workers' compensation protection, or labor protection as employees. Unless specified in your contract, you must also cover your own business expenses. Your rates should factor in these extra expenses.

One of the biggest benefits of working as an independent contractor is flexibility. In most cases, you will be entirely responsible for setting up your working environment and schedule. A client cannot dictate your work hours. This is a sharp distinction to working as an employee, where there may be a reasonable expectation that you will be available during set hours every day.

There is typically a written contractor agreement outlining the work to be done, deadlines, terms, payment (how much, by when, and method of payment), along with details about how either party can choose to end the working relationship.

Deciding Between Employee and Contractor Jobs

There are plenty of reasons and benefits to work as an employee just as there are reasons to work as a contractor. It is important to remember that the company or client has a legal responsibility to hire appropriately. For example, they cannot hire you as a contractor to avoid the additional expenses of hiring an employee if the work situation according to IRS guidelines indicates the job falls under an employee position. This can lead to fines and even lawsuits against the employer.

This is a distinction and one you should review carefully before signing any agreement as an employee or contractor with a particular company.

When to Stay Put

You might not want to make a transition into remote work right away. Perhaps you and your spouse are determining whether or not it makes sense for you to stay in your current role and location while your spouse moves for the military on their own (also known as geobaching). You might be at a base where you are using your present position to gain more experience, earn certifications, or as a placeholder until you move again and get a new opportunity to pursue a different role.

It can take a lot of time to find the perfect remote role, so perhaps you are using this book to prepare your application package well in advance. If you are six months out from a PCS, consider what goals you want to accomplish in your current job and the action steps you want to take to prepare yourself for your next experience. For example, your current employer might help you obtain a meaningful certification that you can use in your current job and that will travel with you as well.

While some companies hire for an imminent start date, it's best to start looking for a remote role at least four to six months ahead of when you are available to begin working in the position. If you get a remote position sooner than expected, you can give your current employer plenty of notice and possibly start working for your new employer before you PCS.

NATO Status of Forces Agreement (SOFA)

Moving around the US for your spouse's military service presents some challenges with remote work, as previously mentioned. Each employer may have specific requirements that exclude hiring in particular states.

However, moving outside the continental US (OCONUS) presents its own unique set of challenges. The NATO Status of Forces Agreement (SOFA) provides for the status of military service members and US civilian employees, and their dependents, who are stationed in NATO partner countries. If you are moving overseas with your spouse to their next duty station, you'll get a SOFA stamp on your passport. You might have heard of this term in relation to a SOFA license, which allows US service members and their families to drive vehicles. However, SOFA is extremely important if you own your own business or intend to work remotely, because you might not be able to continue the work in that OCONUS location depending on the specifics of the individual country agreements.

Your local Military Spouse Professional Network chapter lead or the Military Installations section of Military One-Source can help you determine which local regulations, if any, impact your remote work options.

For example, Germany's SOFA agreement with the US allows military spouses to work in the German economy and for US-based companies, but Italy requires spouses to obtain a work visa. Without that visa, a spouse can lose their SOFA status if they attempt to work in the economy. In short, these rules are very complicated and even working remotely for a US company could trigger SOFA violations for you or legal issues for your employer. Do your research first, especially if your spouse has any say in their next overseas duty station. This might also influence your decision as a couple to consider geobaching if you would have to give up your job or business to go overseas.

As you might expect, if you're allowed to work remotely overseas based on SOFA regulations, you might also face complicated tax situations. Do your research and consider meeting with a financial professional before you move so you have all the facts about how this influences both your career and tax situation.

Once you've evaluated the types of remote work options that align with your current priorities and considered what you need to succeed in a remote position, reflecting on your unique skills, interests, and experiences can help you narrow your search to the best opportunities for you.

Chapter 3 —

Find the Right Work

When starting a career journey, many people think they need to know exactly what their end goal looks like. But before you can know what your end goal of success looks like, you need to determine where you are on your journey, what kind of work you like, what you don't like, and what training or additional learning you might need to succeed in your job search.

The job search process looks different for a younger military spouse thinking about enrolling in education, still earning degrees, or recently graduated than it does for a military spouse with ten years of experience in their field looking for a mid-level or advanced role. Don't try to compare yourself to other spouses who are at different places in their journeys. Spouses earlier in their careers might need to spend more time completing inventories of their skills and interests because they have less work experience to pull from. All too often, remote work is painted as an option for someone at an entry or intermediate level in their career. However, high-level positions are becoming remote at an increasing rate as well. It can take longer to find these kinds of positions since they don't pop up as frequently as entry-level roles like data entry or customer service, but they are out there.

Your mindset is key to how you apply for and land the right job, and it will help you thrive in the right role, too.

Adopt a Growth Mindset

Practically everything about a job hunt makes it easy to focus on the negatives. After all, if you're applying for enough positions, you are opening yourself up to rejection every time you hit "submit" on an application!

The growth mindset, as defined by Carol Dweck, says that some of the most successful people are the ones who believe they have abilities they can develop. A fixed mindset, on the other hand, is often associated with people who believe their abilities and skills are set in time and unchangeable. Dedication and hard work are the qualities people with a growth mindset rely on to help them overcome challenges and develop a lifelong love of learning, both of which are highly desirable qualities in a remote employee.

As a job applicant, approaching things with a growth mindset will help you adapt to an ever-changing workforce where new technology is emerging at a rapid rate. You'll need to adapt and pivot multiple times throughout your career, but you'll also need to take on a growth mindset to figure out which of your skills you want to adapt and which new things you want to learn.

A growth mindset is also extremely helpful as you navigate the world of remote employment, where it can be very

competitive to land a position and you have to showcase your
ability to thrive in a home office as part of a bigger team.

As you go through the following chapters, there might be
ideas that are new to you. You might also discover that you
want to take some time to sharpen your skills or revisit your
career goals. Tap into your growth mindset. This is not a race
and there are no prizes for first place. You will work toward
your remote employment goals at your own pace, even if that
means taking some time for re-education or mentoring before
you are ready to apply for jobs.

Whether you are new to the job market, have been in it
for a long time, or are stepping back into it after an absence,
your best starting point is always based on your personal
skills. Plenty of people struggle with defining their best skills,
especially since military spouses struggle with confidence
in the application process. Taking tests and identifying your
skills will help you build your confidence around what kinds
of skills you should lean into.

Know Your Skills and Interests

If you have been in the workforce for a number of years,
you may already know what skills you have honed in different
positions and what skills you enjoy using in particular work
environments. If you don't have extensive employment experience, "look back" style exercises might be more challenging.

Take a Skills Test

Start with a career aptitude or skills test to narrow down
the fields or job types best aligned with your natural skills.
Even if you have plenty of employment experience, a test like
this can help you get to know yourself better and connect that
data to your search for the right job for you now. Improving
your self-awareness and having data about yourself to check
against job descriptions is invaluable.

There are a number of aptitude tests available for free online. Search for key words or phrases like "skills test," "career test," or "personality aptitude test." Take the tests and complete the questionnaires on a few different sites and compare the data. Try to look at the results objectively. Do they accurately capture some of the skills you think are your strongest? Did any results surprise you? Are there base skills you might be able to use to branch out into a new industry or career field with some additional education? Would you cross any of these fields or jobs off your list?

Follow Your Passions

Now that you've completed an aptitude test and brainstormed some of the no-go careers or job aspects, widen the focus to think about some of your passions that should be added to the list. A few questions to consider:

▷ What industries, topics, or ideas would you still be interested in learning about even if you weren't being paid for that time?

▷ What books or magazine stories draw your interest?

▷ What is a career field you've always wanted to know more about but haven't had the opportunity to explore?

▷ What's something you've always wanted to do, but felt was "out of reach" for you?

▷ Is there a passion you spend personal time pursuing that you could get paid to do?

Even when you're working remotely, it pays to know yourself and the kind of atmosphere where you are most likely to thrive. You can even think back to your days in school to remember your experiences, where you struggled, and where you excelled, to provide excellent clues about your passions.

Review Your Resume for Key Skills

If you don't have a resume, start by creating a list of all the positions you've held, including internships, leadership roles, volunteer positions, or paid employment. Note the key skills you excelled at in each of the positions.

Here is a small sampling of great skills that apply across industries. You might already have these in your list of demonstrated skills. Which of these match your career aptitude test? What other key skills do you have?

▷ Project management

▷ Collaboration

▷ Meeting deadlines

▷ Leading a team

▷ Customer service

▷ Budgeting

▷ Data analysis

▷ Planning

▷ Problem solving

Find the skills that match across your different lists or that resonate with you personally. What jobs leverage those skills? By leaning into your strengths and knowing this before you prepare your resume and cover letter for applications, your job search will be that much easier.

Define Your Unique Value Proposition

Your unique value proposition is the combination of your skills, experience, and aptitude that sets you apart from similar applicants.

In some cases, your potential employer may receive hundreds of applications for one job. Many applicants will have similar skills. Others will be eager to learn. Your challenge is to stand out from the crowd and capture the employer's attention in a meaningful way. A candidate who makes a memorable positive impression will be the one most likely to get the role.

Think about what you bring to the table that is unique. When you get a hiring manager excited about you, that interest may carry throughout the entire hiring process and even into job negotiations. The goal is to get someone in your corner as soon as possible who is your champion inside the company. They will be thrilled when you do well and may be willing to go to bat for you up the chain as the hiring process continues.

Examples of unique value propositions for job applicants:

▷ Bringing X number of years of experience in this specific industry

▷ Adaptable and able to undertake multiple projects with the same level of focus and care

▷ Advanced certifications or training showing a real dedication to the field

▷ Excellent communication skills that help you navigate problematic situations with clients, customers, or coworkers

▷ Unique achievements in past positions that set you up well to excel in this new role

▷ Situations that were heading toward disaster in which you were able to step in and bring a project back on track or to a successful outcome

If you're not sure of your unique value proposition yet, continue working through the questions and exercises in this chapter. Ask a former supervisor or coworker what they loved most about working with you and what they think is your unique value proposition. They might surprise you with an answer you weren't even considering!

Conduct a Past Role Self-Evaluation

A past role self-evaluation will help you confirm where you thrive and which aspects of a job are most important to you. If you've been in the workforce before, the easiest starting point to consider is the jobs you've already had or the industry in which you've worked most recently. While this can represent an easy re-entry or next step when you're moving to a new location, don't limit yourself to career options only because you've done them before and find them to be the most accessible. You'll bring your best to an industry, position, and role when your interests and skills are aligned.

When you first start your search, there are no wrong answers. Your goal with self-evaluation is to narrow down your best options. Once you start applying for jobs, talking with companies, and creating your professional development plan, it will get easier to determine next steps.

This isn't just to help you narrow down your application choices. This exercise will also give you time to reflect and define your thoughts clearly for interviews. A candidate's ability to highlight their past results and analyze what made situations successful or unsuccessful is important for effective interviews. Self-evaluation is not about judging yourself or trying to change core aspects of your personality. It's about finding out what you need to know about yourself to present yourself well and communicate your needs to employers. As you look over past roles, consider a few questions:

- ▷ In what past roles were you the most focused and passionate?

- ▷ What tasks in your various roles were your favorites? Which tasks do you not enjoy?

- ▷ Which tasks called for more skill from you, but you enjoyed learning about them and improving?

▷ Did you prefer working alone or as part of a team?

▷ What kinds of challenges present you with the most fulfillment as you work through and solve them?

▷ What is your strongest form of communication? Does writing or talking energize you more?

▷ How important is it to you to have clear processes, systems, and strategies to follow? If not important, are you the kind of person who wants to have a say in shaping those for you or an entire team?

▷ How important to you are things like promotions and upward mobility within a company?

▷ Are there social justice or environmental values important enough to you that you want to specifically look for a company that matches those values and has specific initiatives?

▷ How do you do with task switching? Would you thrive in a role like customer service where you are involved with numerous different projects and problems throughout the course of the day, or would that feel exhausting to you?

▷ How much mentorship would you like on the job? Is it important to you that you have a direct mentor who works with you regularly?

▷ When you worked on group projects in the past, what kind of a role did you play? Were you happy with this role?

When looking at your past employment experience more closely, look beyond the job titles, industries, or roles. Note the soft skills you bring to a company, such as communication, organization, and collaboration. Brainstorm your soft skills, and keep this list handy.

Assess Professional Development

An issue of natural concern to many military spouses is what to do when they have a dream job or industry in mind but don't feel qualified enough to submit applications in that field due to lack of training or education. If this is where you find yourself, think about what gaps you can close.

Independent learning is a powerful set of skills that shows employers you are driven and willing to take personal initiative. This also helps show you are actively staying current in your field even if you aren't working at the moment. You can proactively frame it as a time of learning to prepare yourself to step into the right role when it comes along.

Online courses, podcasts, books, and other tools can point you in the right direction when it comes to leveling-up your learning. Leaders in your industry might provide certifications or training. These can help you fill gaps in your resume, learn more of the current industry language and approach, and give you material to add to your resume and LinkedIn profile.

Once you have a good sense of where you've been and where you want to go, closing the gap becomes easier. Make a master list of all the resources available to you. There are many organizations for military spouses, education support systems, and networks you can lean into for additional help.

Expect to Like Your Job

These assessments can help you align with a career that is well suited to your values, personality, skills, and interests, but that is just a starting point. You want to enjoy your work. Even if your primary motivation for finding remote employment has to do with securing income for your family, it can be a big mistake to overlook situations that would make you feel unhappy on a daily basis.

There are plenty of books, motivational videos, and blogs out there stating just how important it is to love what you do.

In the best-case scenario, you'll leap out of bed in the morning and race to your desk to get started. But thinking that is the only winning scenario for you could cut you off from situations where you could still find plenty of fulfillment in your work. Having a successful career doesn't require loving every minute of it. Even in a job you love, you will encounter challenges, people who are difficult to work with, budget constraints, leadership problems, and many other obstacles.

At the other end of the spectrum, there are millions of people who hate what they do, who they work for, or who they work with. Set a goal for yourself now that you don't want to end up in that situation, even if you are only showing up for the paycheck. Over time, that kind of career will wear you down, impact your performance, and can even cause problems in your personal relationships due to being angry, exhausted, or overwhelmed (or a combination) all the time.

Think about your least favorite work experience so far. Now remove any aspects like toxic work culture, problematic coworkers, or a bad boss. If you took the specific people you worked with out of the equation, is that job still something you would have been unhappy doing? If yes, make note of what made this position difficult for you so that you can screen job postings, positions, companies, or people that might replicate that experience. If you still loved doing the underlying work, this is a chance to seek out a company with a similar role but a more fitting company culture.

80 Percent Happiness Rule

A personal metric I like to use when looking for a job is the "80 Percent Happiness Rule." Every job, even self-employment, has downsides. Nothing is perfect. When you work as part of a team and collaborate remotely, you don't always get to call the shots or determine what the solution looks like to difficult problems. So the goal is to be at least 80 percent happy in the position and with the tasks, people, and company.

For me, the 80 Percent Happiness Rule is also a metric for reflection. When I've had a bad day, I can reflect on my overall feelings about my job and how much of my time every week I truly feel any type of frustration or deep disappointment with my position. If I'm still happy more than 80 percent of the time consistently—and especially if I'm regularly more than 90 percent happy—it's easy to forget about those other issues.

For example, in a position I otherwise loved, there was one coworker who was difficult to deal with. It was just a personality clash, but their tone and work approach sometimes drove me crazy.

When I stepped back to think about my 80 percent rule, I realized I spent less than two hours per workweek interacting with this person. This person wasn't my direct supervisor, and we didn't collaborate on most of the projects I was responsible for daily. Even though I might internally roll my eyes after this person sent yet another snarky email, I could always reframe and think about how little of my day was impacted by them. Having to cope with someone I had a personality clash with was a small price to pay since it was one of the only downsides of that position.

That was a time when my perspective reminded me of my gratitude for the position, but this rule can also be a wake-up call to leave a position. I recall the first job I had out of college, where I had a coworker who appointed herself my supervisor and was a terrible person to work with. She made mean, condescending remarks, and frequently lied to me and others. Everyone I knew closely in the office had multiple issues with her and actively avoided her. Since I did have to see her and talk to her every day and had multiple bad interactions per week, I ultimately left that job. While the rest of the position brought very low stress to my life, this person was a consistent issue that made the rest of work impossible. In that job, I was about 20 percent happy because this coworker had such a negative impact.

What helps you figure out what 80 percent happy looks like to you? Start a mood tracker for how you feel throughout the workweek; a bullet journal is a great tool to use for this. The 80 percent translates to four out of five days where you feel pretty good to great about your experience and your job.

If you are not currently in the workforce or you plan to re-enter after a long break, give some thought to how you felt about a previous position. Create a pros and cons list. If the cons list is much longer than you realized, you now have a clearer idea of what you want to avoid in a future position.

It's important to think first about what you definitely don't want, because this will help you avoid going further with a job application or interview process when other positive aspects of the job, such as relaxed hours or higher pay, may tempt you into a position where you ultimately would not be happy.

Consider What You Need From a Company

When you are seeking out a remote position, you have to be willing to dig into the company's background to get a good sense of who you'll be working with, the type of team you'll be on, and how team members communicate with one another. Consider aspects like flexibility, room to grow, other benefits offered, and company culture.

Know your flexibility requirements upfront so you can keep them in mind when considering if a company's processes and culture will support what you need. The flexibility of the overall position could be as simple as enabling you to work remotely during traditional office hours in a particular time zone or as flexible as requiring you to log in to complete your shifts a few hours per week. You will find positions all across the board when it comes to a remote opportunity with these parameters in mind.

Landing an opportunity in a company that isn't the right fit for you will only lead to more frustration, even if it does have the advantage of enabling you to work remotely. Remember, this is about your career and your professional development so other aspects of working with a team should be just as important for you. Perhaps you love the fact that a certain company provides additional scholarships and funding for you to get further education. Maybe you are thrilled to find out that every Friday a delivered lunch is sponsored by the company, as well as an opportunity to connect over video to get to know one another better. Decide what is important for you and read between the lines when looking at posted positions. You'll soon be able to tell what the companies you're considering make their top priority. We'll discuss company culture in more detail later, as it is important to assess the culture of an organization before you interview.

See Your Employer's Perspective

Thinking about what makes a position or company the right fit for you is certainly a cornerstone of narrowing your possibilities. Now take what you've learned about yourself and frame that in the context of a potential employer's perspective.

Your employer is looking for the right person for the role and the company. You can help this process by seeking to understand their pain points, challenges, fears, and failures. Help them connect the dots as you answer questions and showcase your expertise and knowledge. Don't try to mold yourself into what you think the employer wants, but it can be a valuable exercise to imagine the pressure points and achievements within the company that have brought them to this point of hiring for this role.

For example, maybe the position you are interested in opened because the sales team at the company has become increasingly successful and overbooked. While this represents good things revenue wise, think about the issues facing the employer right now. They probably want to maintain sales consistency and a great team culture while also expanding to meet increased need. They want to know that the person they hire can jump in quickly and help them grow while also building on the firm foundation that already exists. They might be concerned about hiring someone whose main priority is closing sales to make a commission rather than focusing on what their customer really needs. Learning more about how the company has managed this in the past can help you and them see how you are the best person to move them forward successfully.

After assessing the big picture of your unique skills and passions, and matching what you want from a remote position with the needs of potential employers, you will need to translate all of this to your resume, cover letter, and conversation in your interview.

Chapter 4 —

Craft Necessary Tools

On any journey, you need proper equipment to be successful. If you go on a weekend camping trip without a tent, canteen, cooking utensils, or water, you will likely need to return home early. Likewise, your remote job search is a journey. To prepare, you need to develop the right tools. In this chapter, we'll explore the importance of tools like resumes, cover letters, and the ability to network effectively, as well as common problems that arise as a result of military life and how to reframe them into positives (hello, resume gaps).

Create a Winning Resume

You will need a compelling standard resume that can be repurposed or altered as needed for specific job postings. A standard resume is the foundation for communicating your key skills and experiences. Generally, a resume is a focused summary of your work experience and background relevant to the job of interest. You will use this as your core document and then create new versions to highlight skills or experience applicable to specific positions.

Although you might want to include a range of experience, for most positions, you will focus on the most recent ten years. A longer, more detailed curriculum vitae (CV) that includes all your work experience, certificates, and publications, is common for some industries, such as healthcare or academia. You might also include extensive experience on a federal resume. Otherwise, comb through your past experience to determine what is most relevant to the job at hand.

For military spouses looking for senior-level or executive roles, it is important to update your resume to reflect your management, leadership, and executive experience. Remember that with advanced roles, it's not just about how long you've spent in the industry or position, but about what you achieved. Illustrate how you used your experience to grow professionally and take on more responsibilities.

The following resume sections are listed in the order you should include them on your resume, with the exception of education. There are many reasons to put education at the top under objective or at the bottom. Some industries have particular standards or expectations for resumes. This is a general overview, so be sure to have an industry professional or mentor review your resume as well.

Your Objective

At the top of your resume, list your objective. This is one part of your resume that should be tailored to the specific position you are applying for because it gives the recruiter a quick snapshot of who you are and what you bring. Include career goals and achievements that align directly with the job of interest. Leverage the primary keywords within the job description. Keep this to no more than one or two sentences.

Here's a simple formula to consider:

> I am a (job title/position name) who values (list three soft skills). I bring (X) years of experience in (name top hard skills).

Education

Your education credentials can be placed at the top of the document or at the bottom. Deciding how to format this is based on your personal background and the direct relevance of your education to the role at hand.

If you have already earned a degree, completed graduate work, or earned professional certifications, these are good reasons to highlight your education first. If the job application calls for minimum education requirements you meet, putting this first makes your qualifications clear.

If your education or field of study is not directly relevant to the job, you can put your educational details later. If you have not achieved a bachelor's degree or have limited educational experience, consider placing your education last. This doesn't mean you are lessening the importance of your educational background, rather that you have chosen to highlight other more relevant experience instead.

List each school's name where you completed study (or are currently attending), dates attended, field of study, and degree or diploma received (or expected graduation date). Note any exceptional academic honors or recognition.

Include relevant details about professional certifications, licenses, or continuing education credits, especially those that may be required for performing work in another geographic location. Research these requirements ahead of time so you understand and can present solutions to maintaining qualifications where you will live (and perform remote work).

Skills

Showing a variety of skills on your resume is important, and these are usually presented in different ways.

Hard Skills

Hard skills refer to specific software program proficiencies or industry-specific skills directly related to programs or tools you use on the job. These show your ability to perform specific job tasks and should be listed by name in a skills section of the resume. When possible, match the wording of your relevant hard skills to requirements listed in the job posting. This list is an example of hard skills for a marketing expert:

> ▷ HubSpot marketing

> ▷ Active campaign management

> ▷ Meta Business Suite

> ▷ Data analysis

> ▷ Copywriting

> ▷ Google Ads/PPC

> ▷ Email newsletter management

> ▷ Funnels

Soft Skills

Soft skills are also critical. Many employers are willing to invest in an employee who does not have all the needed hard skills, if that person is a quick learner and brings great soft skills to the table. Soft skills don't belong in the skills section; give preference to your hard skills there. Instead, soft skills should be sprinkled throughout your resume and cover letter, embedded in your job descriptions and achievements.

Examples of in-demand soft skills for remote jobs include:

> ▷ Proactive, clear written and verbal communication

▷ Adaptability

▷ Growth mindset

▷ Exceptional focus and productivity, minimizing distractions

▷ Ability and self-initiative to prioritize, meet deadlines, and manage a variety of projects or tasks

▷ Emotional intelligence

▷ Creativity

▷ Persuasion

▷ Collaboration

Digital Skills

It is especially important when applying for remote jobs that you show you are familiar with and successful in using technology that might come up on the job. Indicating tech savviness reassures your potential employer that you will be able to support your remote environment and adapt easily as technology evolves.

In addition to mentioning digital skills on your resume, listen for clues during interviews to determine which digital skills are most important to the employer. Highlight these with specific examples at that time. Proactively consider situations you may face in this position and how you might approach troubleshooting, or share ways you have addressed similar challenges in the past.

Digital skills a remote employer may look for include:

▷ Technical abilities and willingness to troubleshoot. Without an IT employee in your home office, you'll need to be able to adapt if your computer shuts down unexpectedly, your video software doesn't recognize your audio input, or you lose internet.

▷ Ability to work independently but also contribute as part of a team via electronic communication. While you'll be at home alone in your own office, you'll likely still be collaborating with other team members on a regular basis. Showcase that you're easy to work with, familiar with navigating conflict or misunderstandings, and excited to work as a team targeting similar goals. Acknowledge challenges of virtual or electronic communication, and share ways you work through that.

▷ Self-training and initiative to learn best practices. Whatever your proficiency level in certain software programs or digital platforms, you are likely to encounter times when you need to learn procedures for new projects or after software updates. Explain ways you use online help, manuals, tutorials, and other methods to support yourself in these situations.

▷ Proper digital etiquette. How you conduct yourself on video calls, chats, emails, and other digital platforms reflects on the company. This may impact internal productivity or external brand perception. Go beyond knowing the rules of when to mute, and show your respect for professionalism in digital environments.

▷ Awareness of digital security concerns and willingness to honor safe practices. You may be asked to install special software, log into a Virtual Private Network, or follow certain protocols to protect company files or sensitive data. Your employer needs to know you will safeguard passwords and keep work information separate from other family members' electronic activities.

Recent Work Experience

List your recent and most-relevant work experience for the job at hand. List up to four positions here that are most aligned with the skills and experience you need for this job. Each of these should include your roles, time spent there, and a recap of some of your greatest accomplishments. If you're looking for a managerial role, lean heavily into your accomplishments related to hiring, training, and managing other people either remotely or in a traditional work environment. If you've already done this successfully, it will be more of a seamless transition for you. Whenever possible, use numbers, key performance indicators (KPIs), or other results-focused outcomes in these bullet points.

Under this section where each job has a strong description, you can also include "Other Work Experience" to call attention to summarized experiences (e.g., twelve years as the editor of various publications) or unpaid positions such as volunteer work or internships. Don't list out bullets here; instead, use this space to present a picture of your total time in the workforce.

Awards and Honors

Keep this short and sweet. These are about who you are as a person and your character, allowing the hiring manager to get a more complete picture. This section can also spark some great interview questions. If you struggled to fit all your accomplishments under an individual job listing, consider putting a few here instead. If you don't have any recent awards or honors, skip this section.

Design Tips

Resumes have not changed much in terms of templates or styles for many years. It can be tempting to create a flashy new style as you start this round of job applications. However, heavily-designed resumes are often not the best fit for remote work because complex formatting cannot be easily read or scanned by applicant tracking systems (ATS) or other digital systems, costing you an opportunity even if your skills and resume information are solid.

The focus of your resume should be you and your experience, not distracting colors, fonts, or images. Check out resume templates and see what catches your eye in a quick scan. When in doubt, choose an easy-to-read format. One exception: If you're in a creative field where design and formatting are a chance to showcase your skills, or if the employer has directly asked you to be creative in your submission, you can play around with these concepts.

Resume Length

One of the most common questions applicants have about the process of applying for remote jobs is the length of the resume. You have probably heard the advice that your resume should never be longer than one page. This is often not the case when it comes to remote jobs, and some recruiters are perfectly comfortable looking at a two-page resume.

In fact, using up to a two-page resume gives you an opportunity to present critical keywords and experience that might help get you an interview.

Your resume does not get the job for you. It opens the door to a conversation with the hiring manager and the offer of a job interview. Therefore, you want to make sure it showcases you with your best foot forward. Edit your resume for the length needed to efficiently highlight your best, most relevant experience for this position.

Resume Gaps

One of the biggest challenges for military spouses is handling gaps in a resume. Perhaps your work history is spotty from frequent moves or needing to make changes during a spouse's deployment. Maybe you made an exit and re-entry into the workforce due to having children, caregiving responsibilities, or for physical or mental health reasons. The challenges of military life more often than not create the need for military spouses to address nonsequential work experience.

If there are substantial gaps on your resume, here are a few ideas to keep in mind:

- ▷ Use years rather than specific start/end dates to denote your general work experience.

- ▷ Don't forget about things you did in between, including freelance work, consulting, volunteering, getting certifications, and going back to school. These can help paint an overall picture of other things you were doing during that time.

- ▷ If a time period is not relevant, delete it from the resume. It is completely reasonable to remove things that don't relate to the job application at hand, including positions that aren't directly connected. It's completely normal to have some gaps as you call the employer's attention to your most relevant positions and experience.

One of the best things you can do to address gaps is to leverage the present and future. Set a goal for the next six to twelve weeks of something new you can learn in a virtual training or a place where you can find virtual internships. Then dedicate yourself to completing those projects or programs. This shows your employer that you're committed right now and you have already taken forward action steps.

Emphasizing what you've done or are currently doing to get ready to move back into the workforce or be the best candidate for a particular opportunity can set the tone for your entire resume. It shifts the focus from the past (and gaps) into how committed you are to your current pursuits. Learning new things also shows that you are driven, self-motivated, and care about learning, all of which are valuable to employers.

Resume Coach

Writing your resume on your own is an excellent exercise to help you review the skills that will come up in your cover letter and interviews. However, your resume is also likely to be the biggest obstacle blocking you from getting those coveted invites to interview. If you haven't created a resume in a while or you are unsure about the best presentation of your skills and experience, working with a professional can help you pull it all together meaningfully.

If you choose to hire a professional career coach or resume writer, you will still need to gather the details of your skills and experience first, and be able to clearly communicate your career and remote work goals. When seeking out someone to help with your resume, make sure their experience aligns with your industry, remote work, applicant tracking systems, military spouses, or, ideally, all of these.

Write a Compelling Cover Letter

Just as you will adapt your foundational resume for each job application, you will do the same with your cover letter template.

The same cover letter should not be used for every single job. Swapping out the title and company name is not enough; in fact, each cover letter should be personalized to the job in question. Every letter you send should communicate why you are the right fit for this specific job. Going this extra step shows the hiring manager that you are committed and serious.

Personalizing each cover letter also allows you to pull keywords from the job description to match your experience.

Cover Letter Format

A cover letter should be only a few paragraphs long. This is prime real estate that should focus exactly on the most important points you want to communicate. In the first paragraph, mention the position itself and your unique value proposition that differentiates you from many other applicants.

A simple way to approach this opening paragraph is to talk about, in this order:

▷ The industry you work in

▷ The people you help in your role within that industry

▷ What's unique about you

In your second paragraph, illustrate proof of the claims you make in the first one and in your resume. In five to eight sentences, include details such as:

▷ Examples of how you handled similar tasks and projects in the past

▷ Personal things that make you a good cultural fit for the company

▷ Why you're attracted to this position

The purpose of this second paragraph is for the reader to start imagining what you'd be like on their team and to build their trust that you have the skills to do the job well.

Your final paragraph is the briefest section of your cover letter. In it, include:

▷ A summary statement with your closing thoughts

▷ An invitation for the reader to interview you

▷ A thank you for their time

▷ Your direct contact information

Your cover letter should be brief, but it should give the reviewer a clear picture of who you are and what you have to offer the company in that role. The goal of the cover letter is to pique their interest and encourage them to review your resume in more depth.

Produce a Quality Video

Increasingly, remote roles are using a video submission as the first material they look at either before, during, or after your resume is submitted. This can be asked for at the same time as a cover letter or in lieu of a cover letter altogether. Companies are doing this for two main reasons: many view cover letters as outdated methods of screening applicants and since the role will be remote, it's a good way to get a sense of the applicant's personality and work environment quickly.

Keep in mind these tips when creating and submitting a video to a potential employer or recruiter:

> ▷ Dress for the job you want to have. Dress professionally and avoid loud patterns or distracting clothing.

> ▷ Scan your background before hitting record. Is there anything in the camera's view you don't want in the frame? Remember that employers are not just looking at you but also at your surroundings.

> ▷ Keep your hairstyle and makeup clean and simple; shave or keep facial hair tidy. Stick with a natural approach that will be similar to how you'll style yourself if you're selected for a future interview.

> ▷ Check your lighting. A ring light is a simple, low-cost tool that can help adjust for low light. If you're going to work remotely, it's good to purchase one of these anyway since it will likely become a mainstay in your home office. Avoid dark rooms where your face cannot be clearly seen.

▷ Always record in a professional setting. Unless the company clearly has values of a laid back or casual approach or has specifically asked you not to record in a home office, don't record in your car, a restaurant, or other similar location.

▷ Check the sound environment. Don't record when the air conditioner is running or the clank of the washing machine can be heard in the background.

▷ Give yourself grace. It's okay to record multiple times until you're happy with the result. Very few people get a winning submission video on the first try. If you find yourself getting frustrated with the process, take a quick break to grab a drink of water or take a few deep breaths!

▷ Don't overcomplicate the recording process. You don't need expensive recording equipment; you can use your phone or computer to capture your video. Set aside time to review a few brief tutorials so you feel confident in what you have to say and the recording tech itself.

▷ Avoid sounding like you're reading from a script. You can keep some notes on the screen with any questions the employer has asked you to address or key points you want to hit, but you want to come across as natural as possible.

▷ When recording, keep your eyes focused on the camera. This will help the viewer feel as though you're speaking directly to them.

▷ Aim for your honest personality. If you're bubbly and outgoing, address the key things you need to on the video while also showcasing that personality. Help the employer get a good sense of who you are.

▷ Set aside plenty of time to record each submission video so you feel confident about what you send. Save the file with your name, the date, the company's name, and the job application title.

▷ Remember to store each application video in a convenient place so you can go back and review it before an interview.

Manage Your Documents and Applications

Your resume, cover letter, and application video are tools that open the door for you to advance within a company's hiring process. Take the time to manage these well throughout your job search.

Tips before you submit your documents or application:

▷ Read each of the paragraphs in your cover letter out loud to make sure your message is clear.

▷ Proofread or use a proofreading tool to check for accurate spelling, grammar, and punctuation.

▷ Verify that all your fonts and formatting match throughout these documents.

▷ Save your resume and cover letter in both document and PDF versions (employers tend to ask for one or the other).

▷ Continue to update your resume if your job search is taking some time. New certifications, courses, and experience can be added as you go.

▷ Double check the job listing to make sure you followed all instructions and included the information and formatting as requested.

It's helpful to create a chart or spreadsheet to keep your applications and status organized. Update your sheet with each new submission. Track interviews, rejections, and notes about any feedback you receive. Apply lessons learned to your next submissions.

However you choose to stay organized, be consistent. Since you'll have multiple versions of your resume and cover letter, create a folder system to store for quick reference. For example, you might create folders based on employer and put all documents for that employer in the designated folder.

It will also be helpful for you to use similar naming conventions for your documents so you can find them quickly in a computer search. For example:

YourName-CompanyName-Position-Doc_Date
LauraBriggs-XYCo-Marketer-Resume_08012022

As you apply to similar positions, you can review your other resume and cover letter versions to have a better starting place for customizing them.

Grow Your Network

You've taken the career aptitude tests and reviewed your resume. You have a short list of what you think you want to do. Before applying for jobs or during the interviewing process, you may have questions or concerns that could be answered by someone already in the field. Networking can help you in many different ways as you work toward the remote job of your dreams, including things like:

▷ Finding a mentor or coach to help you at each stage of the application process or to give you insight on a specific aspect of your job search, such as reviewing your resume

▷ Participating in a community of other military spouses or remote job seekers who motivate and encourage each other

▷ Connecting with someone who can give you more insight on their own career trajectory

▷ Getting perspective from recruiters, who might have more awareness of job openings and companies with remote roles

▷ Talking with someone in a field you're interested in to hear their suggestions for closing resume gaps or getting additional training

▷ Shadowing someone during a day in the life of their work to see what it really looks like and their perspective on the pros and cons

Often an overlooked aspect of job hunting, networking with recruiters can give you a head start on applications. Many companies use recruiters to help them fill remote roles, so you'll want to be connected to people who have these leads first and might be able to shepherd your application through the process. Tell the recruiters in your network what you're looking for and what your ideal role looks like. Form relationships with two to three recruiters in industries related to your primary interest so you have a solid pipeline. This is especially important for military spouses seeking high-level positions.

Generally, you'll find two main approaches to networking helpful during a job search. The first is growing your network and connecting with like-minded people or elders in your industry to keep an open line of communication. It's good to nurture this network frequently and update them when you are looking for your next position. The second approach is specifically about this job search. When you're looking for a resume coach, an informational interview, or an introduction, you want to be as clear and concise as possible. Many people are busy, especially if they're already working in a company or organization. Have a clear ask for the person you're contacting.

Clarity Is Key in Networking

Start by doing your research. Don't blatantly ask someone "Can you tell me more about your job?" before you've done some of the legwork to rule out basic questions and consume any other content you can find about this individual and their role. There's a big difference between your first outreach being very generic, vague, and time-consuming for a mentor to read through to try to sort out what you really want and having a specific ask ready for them.

Imagine there's a leader in a nonprofit you greatly admire and you're hoping to work either at that nonprofit or in a similar organization. For so many reasons, it could be beneficial for you to expand your network and reach out to this person. But before doing so, show that you've gone above and beyond. Here's an example of a potential message:

> *Thanks for connecting with me here on LinkedIn, Ms. Terry. I've been a big fan of the work you're doing at [nonprofit name] for years. I read in a recent interview you did that hiring for a nonprofit can be difficult if the applicant just appears to want any job but doesn't have the specific desire to work at that organization.*
>
> *I was wondering if you'd have a few minutes to speak with me about this subject, as I'm currently in the process of applying for nonprofit roles, and I want to show how connected I am to their mission in an authentic way. I don't want hiring managers to think I'm volunteering, donating, or getting involved simply because I want a job.*
>
> *I understand that you're busy, so if you only have a few moments to send me a short response here on LinkedIn, I would still really appreciate*

it. If you have more time, I would love to connect via phone or video chat. Again, thank you for the excellent work you're doing in this field. It's very inspirational.

See how that is so much more targeted than "Can you tell me more about your job?" The ask here is very specific, and the applicant has gone above and beyond in doing their research by reading about this leader. The sender has even given the busy person an "out" by saying that even a short message response would be appreciated. Give your contact a choice. They might not have time to speak with you over the phone or video. If you've really gone above and beyond, such as attending an online summit where they spoke, try to ask your question in that time and then follow up with them personally to remind them of who you are and to thank them for sharing their insights.

Imagine that you get a "Sure, I'll chat with you" response to the thoughtful LinkedIn message. Now it's time to set clear expectations, showing that you'll be respectful of their time. If they ask you to use a calendar link to book time, use it and respect it by showing up prepared and on time. If they ask you to schedule through their assistant, do it. This person is doing you a favor, and the easier you make it for them by respecting their systems and time, the more likely they are to help you.

Here's a good response to an acceptance of your ask:

Thanks so much for your response! I appreciate it. I'll use your link to grab a 20-minute time slot. I have four questions I'd like to ask you. If it would be helpful for me to share those general topics with you or your assistant before we talk, please let me know.

Respect, Respect, Respect

Especially on LinkedIn and in email, thought leaders, business owners, and company executives get bombarded with requests. You might think you are only asking for fifteen or twenty minutes of their time, but consider that they may only have fifteen extra minutes per week and you might be one of twenty people asking for that time.

Check to see if that company has a guide, training, podcast, video, or report available on the topic you're asking about, and if that information is publicly available. Show respect for the networking contact's time by doing this work first. If you can't find the information or still have a question, mention that you did already look for these resources.

As a business owner, I am consistently contacted by well-meaning aspiring contractors or people new to the industry asking if I can call them and give them advice. It's overwhelming and many of the asks are too unclear. If I don't have a sense of what the call is about or have clear parameters for how long I will be on a call, I usually have my administrative assistant decline. When the ask is very clear and I can tell this person is a reader of one of my books, one of my course students, or otherwise stepping a bit above and beyond in their ask, I am much more likely to respond positively and do what I can to help them.

As you're networking and meeting new people, don't forget about people in your past who can help you as you apply for new roles, such as those who could serve as references.

Reframe Military-Related Job Changes

The hiring manager for the job you want may not understand the challenges you face as a military spouse. Or your potential employer may think you are a job hopper since you've changed positions often; they may wonder if you are worth considering if you'll only be around for a few years. Perhaps you have worked jobs you were overqualified for because that is all that was available at a particular duty station. For these reasons, you may be tempted to conceal your military affiliation since it can be viewed by employers as a negative.

It is up to you whether or not you mention your status as a military spouse. Keep in mind this could likely be discovered with a quick social media scan, and you don't want a potential employer to think you are trying to deceive them.

The bottom line is that no interview or job offer should hinge on your status as a military spouse. The focus should be on your skills, qualifications, and ability to bring great things to that company. Try to shift your mindset and the conversation with your prospective employer back to your unique value proposition.

In addition to everything else you offer, your experience serving as a military spouse affords you an array of skills that can be beneficial to any employer. Proactively think about what skills make you unique because of that role. We often think of the military impacting our careers in a negative way, but if you reframe this, you can showcase how being a military spouse makes you stand out from other applicants.

Here are just a few examples of skill sets that military spouses excel at or have fine-tuned due to a military lifestyle:

▷ Organization. Military families are often able to manage their lives and families through major disruptions, schedule changes, duty station changes, new homes and neighborhoods every few years, and major shifts during long-term training, sea duty, or deployment.

▷ Inclusivity. Being able to communicate clearly, succinctly, and to a broad audience of many types of people is a powerful skill. Given that you've probably interacted with people of all different backgrounds, military ranks, and cultures, you bring an inclusive and welcoming perspective to the table.

▷ Resourcefulness. Military families are excellent problem solvers, viewing situations as having many possible solutions they are willing to explore in response to an obstacle.

▷ Empathy. As part of a distinct community, military families can deeply empathize with others who are facing challenges, often making them empathetic and caring managers, coworkers, and customer-facing employees.

▷ Unflappability. Military families often face situations that are well beyond what many civilians encounter (long periods spent away from a spouse, the stress of a spouse's dangerous day-to-day job, professional composure at formal events and in the public eye, caregiving the mental and physical injuries of a servicemember spouse, and more). It takes a lot to rattle military spouses. Their tolerance can be much higher before they feel stress, anxiety, or frustration on the job. This means you can position yourself as a cool, calm, collected person at work who will greatly contribute to team culture.

When explored in this way, it's easy to see how you can shift the focus from an employer's fear of negative things (like you leaving in a few years or being unfocused when your spouse is on deployment) into a positive conversation around how your role as a military spouse is like a career in and of itself where you've honed some significant soft skills.

Likewise, if you have jobs on your resume for which you were overqualified, think about why you pursued that work, such as to continue earning an income, try out a new career field, or develop professionally. Reframe the statements you make to address those situations. Being a resourceful worker who believes in making a contribution and values hard work is a good quality for an employer to hear. Practice answering interview questions with these ideas in mind.

Understand Applicant Tracking Systems

No discussion of remote job applications would be complete without covering the impact of hiring tools known as applicant tracking systems (ATS). If you've actively been applying to remote positions and receiving no callbacks or interview requests, it is possible that the ATS employers are using is working against you.

As employers receive more and more applications in a competitive job market, many have turned to applicant tracking systems as one way to streamline the hiring process. An ATS enables employers to implement the screening of resumes and cover letters before they reach the desk of a human for a personal review. If you are under the impression that your biggest obstacle to getting a job with your dream company is getting the attention of a recruiter or hiring manager, you are missing out on this important component that is especially key for remote jobs: passing through ATS.

Large corporations, mid-size and small businesses, as well as nonprofits filter resumes through the ATS process. So it is critical that you understand how to tailor each of your resumes to make it through this initial screening round.

How ATS Works

Software for applicant tracking systems allows employers to use hiring and recruiting tools to sort through thousands of resumes. Whether or not your resume is ever seen by the hiring manager could depend entirely on how well you adjusted it for that particular job. In the past, many people approached writing their resume based on an industry as a whole. For example, someone with experience in marketing would include plenty of industry terms and buzzwords related to marketing.

However, companies use different descriptions of tasks within particular job listings. Top employers hire for multiple jobs at the same time and receive hundreds or even thousands of resumes for every opening. ATS weeds out unqualified applicants by searching for specific skills that match the job.

If your resume has not been adapted for the individual job at hand, you may not make it through the initial ATS filter. While this process does help an employer narrow the applicant pool, top candidates can slip through the cracks and miss the important opportunity of getting to the next step in the review process with a recruiter or hiring manager.

One recent study found that the vast majority of large corporations leverage applicant tracking systems. Another found that up to 98 percent of Fortune 500 companies use ATS, and 35 percent of small organizations leverage the software as well.

Not only is ATS the first receipt of your application, your resume may be stored there long after your original submission. Hiring managers and corporate recruiters can return to the submitted resumes to sort through them in a number of different ways depending on the software program they are using. While some recruiters might look at every single application that comes through the ATS, many conduct a quick glance to determine which may be worth a second look.

Your resume may have only six seconds to grab the attention of a hiring manager glancing over it. This makes it even more critical for your qualifications and top skills to be identified clearly at the top. Certain systems rank your resume in comparison to the job description and use a percentage score to determine how well your resume matches up.

What's frustrating is that if you have listed your skill as "project management" and the job description includes the term "project manager," the ATS might not pick up that these are referring to the same skill set. But the good news is you don't need to match 100 percent to the description. The sweet spot is an 80 percent match between the job description and your resume.

How Recruiters Use Keyword Searches

Recruiters can filter resumes in an ATS by searching for key titles and skills. For example, imagine that a recruiter is attempting to hire an executive assistant. A search within the ATS for the term "executive assistant" would reveal only those people who have worked in that specific job before. Anyone who does not have that term in their resume could miss out on being categorized as a match.

The best way to determine which keywords and skills you need to include in your individual resume is by analyzing the job description closely. There are also free tools available to help you see how closely your resume matches a particular job description. Search online for "ATS tools for resume writers."

For the best chance of matching, you will need to create a tailored resume for every job you apply for. However, if you are applying to dozens or hundreds of jobs, it might not be practical to tailor an individual resume for each specific position. During the application process, if you see a job that is with your dream company or sounds like the perfect opportunity for you, prioritize your efforts for personalization there.

Importance of Formatting

One other thing to keep in mind after you have analyzed the skills and keywords to include in your resume is the importance of proper formatting. Since applicants will be submitting dozens or hundreds of different types of formatted resumes into the system, some ATS software programs take this document and translate it over to a digital profile to make things more easily searchable by the recruiter. This can be a significant problem if you have over-formatted your resume.

Because ATS often have unintelligent or outdated algorithms, your information might be lost in translation. If vital details or keywords are not imported over in the system, your most-important information or top qualifications won't show up for the recruiter at all. Although applicant tracking systems are constantly being improved, building significant formatting into the document increases your risk of losing key details.

There is no one-size-fits-all answer to how to adapt your resume for ATS. The importance of adapting your resume for these individual positions is to make it through the initial screening process to open the door to a possible job interview. Here are the top tips to increase your chances of making it through the majority of ATS programs:

▷ Tailor your resume to the top jobs in your search list using keyword tools.

▷ Save each of your files with a .docx extension as this is the easiest way to format over to other preferred options if needed. Save the name with the company you are applying for so if you are contacted for an interview, this information is easily found.

▷ Avoid using headers or footers as these can cause formatting issues.

Your resume and cover letter are living documents. Don't forget to edit your resume as you take on new work or volunteer experience or you finish certifications.

Chapter 5 —

Search, Apply, Repeat

N ow that you know the kind of remote employment you are looking for and have developed the skills and necessary tools for your remote job search, it's time to begin the application process. Applying for any job is a difficult process and one that can take longer than you expect. It's important to have the right mindset going in and clear expectations of what might happen in this process, so you feel confident and motivated to push forward. In this chapter, we'll discuss more about how and when to apply for positions and how to set yourself up for success in a coveted interview.

The Application Process

Perhaps one of the most frustrating parts of applying for any job is not knowing exactly how long it will take for you to get an interview, much less an offer, from a company. Remote work has a very competitive job landscape with people all over the country or world applying. And some industries have fewer remote jobs available than in-office jobs, which may further extend the hiring timeline.

When I put my resume on the remote work job market, it took a full six months from the time I started seriously applying until I accepted an offer with a company. During that time, there were two other instances where I made it to the final round of interviews, one which ended in an offer I did not accept and one in which another person was selected for the job.

Over the course of this period, I experienced every emotion imaginable in the job-hunting process, from excitement to nerves to feeling frustrated that I wasn't making further progress. I share this to say: If it takes you some time to find a situation that's the right fit for you, that's normal. This process takes time even after you develop an incredible cover letter, resume, and job application strategy.

How Employers Talk About Remote Work

Not every employer talks about remote work in the same way. When you're visiting jobseeker sites and trying to sort results, you will find that some companies use a dropdown category for remote jobs, but many do not. Be prepared to research with a variety of terms, such as:

- ▷ Job offsite
- ▷ Work offsite
- ▷ Distributed team
- ▷ Remote available
- ▷ [City/Location Name] or Remote
- ▷ Telework
- ▷ Work from home

- ▷ Virtual job

- ▷ Virtual work

- ▷ Work from anywhere

- ▷ Online

When searching on major job boards, look for all of these terms so you see as many opportunities as possible. Be aware: Some of these same terms are used by scammers, especially "work from home."

Within these job postings, read through all the details. Some may note a veteran-friendly position or that the company gives preference to veterans. These clues can help you determine to what extent you want to spotlight your role as a military spouse.

Avoid Scams

To avoid a scam job, look for signs to determine legitimate opportunities. A legitimate employer will:

- ▷ Be easy to find on a company website and will usually have a presence on LinkedIn. Look for employees who list working at this company; their profiles should be complete with a picture.

- ▷ Use a professional email address that usually ends in @companyname.com

- ▷ Be willing to speak with you by phone or video.

- ▷ Never ask you to pay for or buy anything before you get a job offer.

When it comes to scam jobs, if your gut is telling you something is off, you're probably right. Be more cautious of providing any personal information like your address, scans of your driver's license, and official paperwork that has your Social Security number on it.

There are plenty of scams out there, but some of the most common for military spouses include promises of administrative assistant or bookkeeping work that involves a flat weekly payment for very little work. Another red flag is if someone asks you to buy equipment that you'll later be reimbursed for or when the employer asks for you to send upfront cash.

Early in my remote work career, I had a legitimate client who needed me to use a certain printer and postage machine to mail his marketing campaigns. He bought both of them and shipped them to me. Unlike a scam, I didn't have to buy the equipment and wait for someone whose business I couldn't find online to pay me back. Even if I hadn't already had a working relationship with him, I could find his website, phone number, and other contact details easily, and his company had multiple online reviews. This example shows that it can be hard to tell when someone is legitimate or not, but there are common warning signs. Keep in mind that if you will work as an independent contractor instead of as an employee, you may be required to supply your own equipment. But that does not involve giving money to a company in order to get the job.

Where to Find Jobs

Many of the traditional job search options still apply when seeking remote work, but there are also a few specific places that cater to remote work and military spouses.

Associations and websites that curate information and send daily email digests or jobs listings specific to your industry help maximize efficiency during a remote job search. A few examples to try: FlexJobs, Remote.co, Virtforce, Grow with Google, Military Spouse Employment Partnership, LinkedIn, Indeed, AngelList, The Mom Project, career pages for specific companies, and plenty more!

Since there are so many places to potentially find job leads and great positions to apply for, it helps to break down the process into small steps you can accomplish on a weekly basis. Being consistent every week will help get you to your goal.

Set a Schedule for Applying

Plan to apply to a minimum of ten positions per week when you are actively looking for a remote job. If you have time to apply to more than this without sacrificing the quality of your application materials, do so. Job opportunities can be posted any day of the week, so there are a few ways to schedule this process as you go:

> ▷ Gather information on interesting positions on Monday and Tuesday and spend the rest of the week applying to those jobs.

> ▷ Scan daily for new jobs on various job board sites, making notes about which ones you want to apply to immediately and which ones could wait a few days.

> ▷ Check out one to two sources of job leads each day and apply directly to those as you discover them.

Set a schedule that works for you, based on when you have time to focus with the least distractions or interruptions. Using your best thinking time to fill out applications and update your resume or cover letter will help you avoid mistakes that can jeopardize the success of your application.

Capture Job Data

Being organized and persistent are the two most important qualities of applying for remote positions. Some companies have a very long application process and might come back to you many weeks or even a few months after you initially submit your information. As you apply, make it easy for yourself to refer back to what you've already sent and gather data on where you're having the most success or struggles. A spreadsheet is a good way to track and update as you go.

A cloud-based folder of information related to each company and job is helpful too. By the time someone reaches out to you about an interview, job listings may be removed from the company website, so you want to keep a copy for reference.

Some of the critical information you'll want to store as you apply so you can easily and quickly find it later:

▷ Name of position

▷ Company name

▷ Date applied

▷ Date of response or interview

▷ Point of contact/email, if any

▷ Link to job description in your folder

▷ Link to resume used for this application

▷ Link to cover letter used for this application

It's easy to assume in the moment that you'll remember, but you won't once you are fifty applications deep and can't even remember what you submitted. Keep it organized and easily searchable.

Remember to come back to your spreadsheet as you hear back from companies. Note where you advanced to the next round or any other notes from direct contact with them. Some companies take a few months to review all materials and contact applicants, whereas others take action in a few weeks. Some companies only contact you if they are interested.

When a Company Reaches Out

Each company has a different approach to the hiring process, especially when it comes to remote jobs. Some might ask you to submit a brief video or fill out a longer application or submit test results. Be prepared for this variety of requirements. Check your email spam folder and your voicemail box regularly so you don't miss anything from these companies.

If you receive a notice from someone at the company, such as a hiring manager, follow the steps outlined in their message. If contacted by email, reply to the message to confirm receipt and that you understand the instructions. Make it easy for the company to see that you are a great communicator already.

If there are any deadlines around the next steps they have requested, make a note of these and adjust your schedule accordingly. Return any requested materials as soon as possible to show that you are still very interested in the job.

Assess Company Culture

No matter how much you want a remote job, it can be hard to remain patient while searching for the right remote position for you. But don't skip this step. Just as you'd be miserable in an office job where the team culture is stressful, toxic, or demeaning, you want to be careful about what kind of remote culture the company you're applying to is consciously building.

Company culture refers to the values, characteristics, and team style of an organization. These factors influence what it's like to work for a particular company. Throughout the application process, gather as many clues as possible about each company's culture. A remote work culture relies on the shared values, respect, and communication styles of all employees and the leadership of the company.

How to Research Company Culture

Before an interview, find out as much as you can about the company as well as the person you'll be interviewing with or reporting to. Be careful to keep this as informational research, not anything that would make the interviewer uncomfortable. For example, you may have good intentions of getting to know more about a person, but reviewing their personal Instagram account and commenting on their photos is going too far.

Look for mentions about the company online. You can set up alerts to receive news about the company. Read reviews on Glassdoor to see what other employees say about working there. Bear in mind that the people most motivated to leave an online review of a company are those who have had a negative experience, and reviews are highly subjective. However, if you spot that the company you're researching has dozens of comments making similar claims and all of them are relatively recent, this is powerful information to know. Check out employees on LinkedIn to see their average tenure with the company and if they've had multiple roles there, as this could give you clues about retention and opportunities for promotion.

You can use this process to determine any red flags. It can also help you think about questions you want to ask during the interview. For example, if you see patterns in employee reviews saying that management doesn't support or mentor employees, you can respectfully ask during the interview what type of mentoring and coaching employees receive from their direct managers. Ideally, the answers will address your concerns.

A few other ways to find out more about a company and its culture:

> If the company has a podcast or the founder/ executives have been interviewed on other podcasts, listen to a few episodes. You can learn a lot about someone's business philosophy this way.

> Has the founder been interviewed by any trade publications or magazines? Read those articles.

> What values does the company list on its website? What else can you learn about the history or team?

> Are there any photos of team retreats or activities?

> Review the benefits section of the job description for hints at company culture, such as annual work

anniversary gifts, team outings paid for by the company, or generous paid time off.

▷ Read employee or team bios. Are they focused entirely on what they do at work or do they give a glimpse into the hobbies and passions this team has outside the workplace? Do the people seem happy?

Being offered an interview or a position for a remote job is especially exciting for someone who has been on the job market for some time, but carefully weigh the pros and cons internally and with anyone important to you. Consider whether this opportunity is the right fit for your goals and your family's situation. For example, if an employer expects that you'll travel to monthly live events, and that doesn't fit with your family's needs due to the military, be prepared to discuss the situation or ask for further details about other options.

Unless there are glaring issues that you discover during this company culture research process, give the team a chance. If you have concerns, however, continue to look for clues as your application advances and especially when you get to the interview stage. You might realize that your interpretation of a workaholic company culture was not true at all. Use all the data to decide when something just isn't a fit for you, but try to give the company the benefit of doubt first.

As a military spouse, a work culture that's welcoming of your unique need for flexibility might be at the top of your list. Make sure you're stepping into an environment where you'll be appreciated, encouraged, and supported. If someone makes statements about political or military issues to you during the hiring process and the content of the comments make you uncomfortable, it might not be the right fit for you.

Although it's hard to turn down an offer of a position or decide not to proceed with the interview process when you note some obvious red flags, it will also be that much better when you do find a position where you are paid well for tasks you love and a team you enjoy working with.

Manage Realistic Expectations

Understanding the process of searching for a remote job can help you frame this process appropriately and keep yourself from getting discouraged when things don't seem to be unfolding as you expect.

I remember my frustrations when I first began my remote job hunt as a military spouse. I assumed that with eight years of freelancing experience as well as advanced degrees, it would be easy for me to find a position that not only aligned with my skills but gave me the opportunity and room to grow, all while working from a remote office.

What I found is that remote positions are extremely competitive. I also found that there are many companies interested in hiring military spouses and supporting the veteran community, so it is in our best interest to showcase our connection to this community and leverage it in the best possible way.

I also learned that the road to the right remote position can be long. Remote job seekers need to be prepared for the entirety of the process and recognize that they might not be able to find a job next week, next month, or even a few months from now. During the six months of my remote job hunt, there were multiple times I was considered for a position and then not contacted again, or interviewed and moved all the way to the final interviewing round before someone else was chosen. There were many pitfalls along the way, but I eventually landed an offer that met my expectations with a team I really wanted to join.

Be Patient and Responsive

One of the things that stood out to me from my remote work job hunt was how long certain hiring processes took.

Many companies held multiple interviews with members of the leadership team and staff. One job application process stretched over the course of four months.

It can be disheartening when a job you think is a sure thing doesn't pan out or when a process you thought would go faster ends up taking a much longer period of time. Be responsible, proactive, and responsive on your end. If you are offered an interview, schedule it as soon as possible to keep things moving forward.

Set Milestone Goals

At the beginning stages of the process, you'll want to carve out time for evaluating your resume, potentially connecting with career coaches, and creating materials such as a professional portfolio, LinkedIn profile, and cover letters that can be repurposed. While we discussed the ins and outs of creating those materials in the last chapter, now is the time to actually make time to do it all.

You'll also spend time setting up your systems for how often you'll search for jobs; the websites, tools, and communities you'll use to do that; and how you'll track this information. It can be a part-time job in and of itself to be scanning for jobs, sending applications, and following up on previous communications with companies. It's a good idea to build this into your expectations and your schedule that you will be spending at least five to ten hours a week on the job hunt.

Committing to a regular schedule is critical for finding and getting the right job for you. So many factors can influence how long it takes to find a good fit, but being consistent will ensure you have cast a wide net for employment opportunities and will have options to choose from. This is especially important for military spouses seeking senior- or executive-level remote roles. Create a calendar for yourself and mark off the milestones of this process, with goals for each step .

Know Your Parameters

The right position may not be the first one offered to you. Rejection is hard, but so is turning down a job offer. During a long job hunt, it can be tempting to take an offer even though it's not your ideal position. Keep an open mind, but also know your minimum requirements for an acceptable position. Define what you are and are not willing to compromise if you are faced with an offer that's not your most ideal.

For example, you may be willing to take a role that is junior compared to your experience if the company has a history of promoting from within during the first year of employment. In that case, you may be willing to start in a lower position or salary level with the intent of moving up in the company.

Early on in my remote work job hunt, I was very clear about what I did and didn't want out of my ultimate position. As a freelance writer for eight years, I had already worked nine-hour days writing, and I was frankly burned out. I received an offer with good pay, but they requested that I be available to write up to 50 hours per week. I turned down that opportunity because it wasn't in line with my vision. Even though it felt crazy to say no to an opportunity, I knew it wasn't the right fit, and ultimately, I was glad I held out for something more in line with what I wanted.

Chapter 6 —

Ace the Interview

W hile the application process can seem daunting and like a job all on its own, the reward comes when you get a response. Sure, that response may not lead to an offer—or an offer you want to accept—but it is a nice way to acknowledge that you did the right things to get a company's attention. Once you've had your momentary celebration, it's time to get back to work.

There's plenty of pre-work to be done before your interview is scheduled. If you want to be on top of things, you can do some of this prep work before you start your job search.

Clean Up Your Online Presence

It's possible that once you get through an applicant tracking system and land in a hiring manager's inbox, their next step will be to look at your LinkedIn or social media profiles.

Thoroughly review and clean up your accounts, especially if you share a lot of personal information, political views, or other material that might not be a good representation of your work persona. Social media, websites, blogs, podcasts, videos, and other online materials can be easily found by most people. Even if your account is a personal one, that doesn't mean it is all private. Some posts may be seen by a mutual connection or reposted in some fashion. It's not enough to clean this once: determine your strategy for consistently maintaining a good professional online representation.

If your main profile picture is or has previously been you with your spouse in uniform, your military affiliation is public. This may also be revealed through comments on your posts. Think carefully about whether or not this is something you want an employer to know about you before the interview. For example, maybe you prefer to focus initial conversations around your skills and unique abilities. Then once the employer knows how great you'd be in the role, they may be more likely to work with you on any flexibility you need due to your military life.

If you leave your military details easily accessible online, it may potentially impact your applications if the employer has misconceptions about the military or assumes you aren't a fit for remote work in the event you have an overseas duty station coming up. This can stop you from going further in the process or even getting to the stage of discussing your skills. Of course, you might not want to work for such a company anyway if they are not already military friendly.

At the very least, clean up any questionable pictures, memberships in public groups that raise questions or concerns, or anything else that doesn't put you forward in the best light. These are best practices for the long run, but essential before you actively apply and interview for positions.

You only get one chance to make a first impression, so if you've piqued an employer's interest with your great resume and application materials, you don't want that hard work to go to waste due to social media profiles or websites that don't represent you well.

Prepare for the Interview

Delivering a winning interview comes down to knowing yourself well, being professional, and preparing yourself for an effective conversation through research, reflection, practice, and other relevant preparation.

Know Your Personality Type

In addition to asking for basic application materials, employers may ask you to take tests that show your personality type and how you work best. Myers-Briggs, DISC, and Clifton StrengthsFinder are common examples. Consider taking one or more of these when you take the skills tests discussed earlier. Store your results in the same folder with the rest of your job application materials so you can reference them before your interview, if needed.

Even if an employer does not request them, these are great tests for any job seeker to take. They can tell you a lot about your work style, making it easier for you to determine if a company culture is the right fit for you. Furthermore, you can use this information to answer questions about your strengths and weaknesses.

Present Your Best Interview Space

In addition to traditional things an employer or hiring team looks for during an interview, remote interviewees have the added pressure of showing, live, that you have the right setup and ability to work from home in a professional office space. While asking you interview questions, they will also take notice of the cleanliness of your interview space, ways you've taken care to minimize disruptions, as well as your lighting, Internet connection, and video quality.

Practice for Interviews

There are many websites with sample interview questions that help you prepare effective responses. Practicing these can build your confidence with your interviewing skills overall and help jog your memory during an actual interview if you get a similar question. Here are a few ways to get that practice:

▷ Run a practice online video call interview with a friend or another military spouse to ensure you can connect, are easily seen on screen, and have working audio. Record the call as you answer some practice questions and review it later. This can help you spot body language cues or other habits you'd like to work on, such as not overusing "so," "um," or "well."

▷ Cut up a list of interview questions and put them in a bowl. Watching yourself in a mirror, practice answering one or two questions at a time. Do this until it becomes second nature for you to answer questions clearly and effectively.

▷ Look up interviews other people have done and determine what you like or don't like in their questions and answers. Your preferred style will emerge from this kind of research.

Use a Behavioral Formula

Many companies use what's called behavioral interviewing, a process of using your past behavior in specific situations as an indication of how you might handle similar challenges in the future. This is an effective way for an employer to see your natural skills in action and for you to showcase your experience in context.

When answering an interview question, focus on a few key details that illustrate your behavior in a specific situation and show your strategic thinking in the way you carry out tasks and approach challenges. Start by describing the situation or circumstance you were in and the obstacles you faced. Provide the most pertinent information about why this situation was important. Do not use generalized examples of things you have done in the past or hypothetical situations.

Any relevant event, including past volunteer experience and situations from a previous job, can be brought up as the first part of your answer. The second step is to discuss, in appropriate detail, the action you took to address the situation. Keep the primary focus on how you adapted, problem solved, communicated, or collaborated to accomplish the outcome. The specific steps you took and your contribution are most important for the interviewer to hear.

Finally, discuss the end result. What were you able to accomplish? What did you learn? How did you influence other team members? Make sure the result you share has multiple positive outcomes as this is the easiest way to illustrate how you operate on the job. Paint a clear enough picture for the interviewer to imagine you being in a similar situation in your role at their company.

Here's an example for a graphic designer role:

> *Interviewer*: Tell me about a time a client was unhappy with your work.

> *Applicant*: A few years ago, I was working on a logo project where the client gave no clear instructions or direction. I used creative license and, unfortunately, the client wasn't happy with the end project. I realized that if I had provided examples of the direction I was thinking much earlier in the process, this might have sparked a

shared creative vision. I listened to that client's feedback and created a revised logo that met their needs. After that, I started using welcome packets with clients that included examples of various branding directions to help them narrow down their design likes and dislikes related to the intended use of their brand.

In this example, the applicant explained a mistake they made, but also used this to showcase their problem solving both in the moment and in the way they developed a system from that experience to prevent problems in the future. Hearing that story, the employer gets an idea of how the applicant might work as part of their existing team, since this example shows initiative, personal accountability, and willingness to create solutions. Whenever possible, steer an interview question back to a positive aspect of your personality and skills.

Prepare for Common Interview Questions

In addition to examples of your skills and past experiences that demonstrate why you are a good fit for a position, be prepared to answer some of the most common general interview questions, such as:

- ▷ Why should we hire you?
- ▷ Why are you leaving your current position?
- ▷ What are your career goals?
- ▷ Where do you see yourself in two to five years?
- ▷ Tell me about the best job you've ever had.
- ▷ Tell me about how you receive instruction and feedback best.
- ▷ What are your strengths and weaknesses?
- ▷ Why is our company the right place for you?

Re-Highlight Skills in the Conversation

All that time you put into editing your resume and preparing it for submission to the job brought you to this interview, but don't assume that the hiring manager or person conducting the interview has read any of your material thoroughly.

Most interviewers glance at it quickly, relying on a human resources team member or ATS to do the initial screening of any application materials. For that reason, imagine that the interviewer has only glanced at your resume prior to your conversation. Don't worry about repeating yourself. Instead, decide ahead of time two to three things from your resume or cover letter that you'd like to make sure get brought up in the conversation. If your interview is virtual, consider adding these skills or examples to a sticky note in your line of vision as you do the interview to remind you.

Prepare Your Own Questions

An interview is a two-way conversation. You will have a chance during or at the conclusion to ask any questions you want of the employer. Here are a few questions you should consider asking the interviewer if they don't come up organically in your conversation:

- ▷ Can you tell me more about what factors go into considering someone for a promotion? Do those review periods happen on a regular basis?

- ▷ How does the company support the professional development of their team?

- ▷ Do you have any tips on communication strategies that seem to be working really well with the team right now?

- ▷ Are there any books, tools, or strategies I should read up on to become more familiar with how this team works?

> ▷ What does a typical week in this position look like?

> ▷ What is your overall time frame for filling this position?

> ▷ Can you tell me more about employees who have been successful in similar positions? Did they have any characteristics in common?

Practice Positive Closing Remarks

At the end of the interview, you have a chance to leave a good impression no matter how the conversation has gone. Whether you felt nervous or rushed, or have any concerns about how you presented yourself, or you are really excited and eager to move forward, take a deep breath to calm yourself. Then take the opportunity to provide a good closure.

Practice a few different closing questions or remarks before the interview, so you've thought through how you might close on a positive note. For example:

> ▷ Is there anything we discussed that I can clarify for you or expand on in order to positively impact my opportunity to continue as a candidate?

> ▷ Is there anything else I can share with you to show my strong interest in this position and my ability to do a great job for this company?

> ▷ I want to express my sincere appreciation for your time and the opportunity to talk about this position. Our conversation has given me even more confidence that my [skills and experience] in this [position] at [this company] are a great match. I want to reconfirm my interest, and I look forward to the next step.

Even if you aren't sure this is the right position or company, or that the interview went well, leave the door open. It may have gone better than you think. And further interviews may reveal more positive details. In fact, a first interview may be with a human resources person or recruiter, and you want the chance to meet with the people you'd actually be working with on the job. Also, this recruiter may be hiring for other positions as well and will remember your professionalism. Prepare to always end on a positive note.

Handle Difficult Questions

Unfortunately for military spouses, some of the most difficult aspects of interviews relate to questions that are directly connected to military life and its impacts on your life. Being prepared for these questions will make it easier to answer them on the spot.

Where do you see yourself in five years?

This is a question that can be frustrating for experienced military spouses who have learned that life and plans can change on a dime. Most military families, at best, only have a general sense that they might be moving in the next couple of years. Beyond that, it's hard to speak to exactly what your professional life will look like.

When asked this question, focus on your answer as if everything in your professional life were within your control. For example: "Over the next five years, my goal is to continue growing as a project manager, obtain my PMP certification, and attend an industry conference as a speaker. I also hope to grow within my role and manage more direct reports."

Are you married to a service member? Are you pregnant?

These and similar questions are illegal. However, that does not mean every employer understands that or won't find a way to work it into the conversation. It's very possible these questions will come up in the interview process, so you have a few choices in that moment:

▷ Point out that these are inappropriate, which could shift the tone of the interview very quickly.

▷ Answer these questions honestly and bring the focus back to your skills and experience.

▷ Ask questions in return to determine and address the real concerns.

If you are seven months pregnant and that is visible during an interview, the answer may be obvious, but an employer still should not be asking about your pregnancy. Perhaps there is an important imminent deadline the person in this position will be responsible for and the employer is concerned that hiring you means missing that deadline since you would be on maternity leave. You might share your desire to work with a company that values a holistic approach to hiring the right people, knowing that at any given time a team member could need to take personal leave for a variety of health or other personal reasons. Perhaps ask how the company supported employees who needed temporary time off during the pandemic. Or ask upfront about the timeline for onboarding and major projects and reassure them you would have a solid plan in place prior to being temporarily on leave. Steer the conversation back to you being the best candidate well beyond one project.

It looks like you move around a lot and change jobs often. Can you tell me more about that?

This is another way of getting into the general questions about your military affiliation, but it's also possible that your prospective employer is asking because there are gaps in your resume. A simple way to address this is by responding, "Yes, my spouse's career gives us the opportunity to move around. It's one of the reasons I'm seeking a permanent remote position with a company I'm excited about working with for the long term."

This answer takes the conversation away from things you can't control (your spouse's job demands) and back into talking about you, which is what the interview should be focused on, anyway. You can "reclaim control" of many interview questions by steering them back to the most important aspects: you and your skills.

Here's another way to address this: "Yes, for several years I've had to exercise more flexibility in my career due to the demands of my spouse's job. Now, however, I'm ready to build on my experiences in a long-term position where I can thrive and really contribute to a company."

What are your biggest weaknesses?

Answer this question honestly, but see if you can bring it back around to something that's also a strength of yours. As an example, the Clifton StrengthsFinder tells you the top five strengths and how you can leverage them to your advantage, but this methodology goes a little deeper when you consider that your strengths have both balconies and basements. Balconies are when those strengths are performing in an optimal way, contributing positively to your life. Sometimes, however, these strengths can take you into a basement, meaning that your biggest strengths can also be your biggest weaknesses.

Here's an example of how a person who has a great ability to focus and scores highly in that category on the StrengthsFinder might respond: "My biggest strength is my ability to focus on difficult problems and work toward solutions while shutting out distractions. However, in some team settings, that can be a weakness if I don't balance that focus time with enough collaboration with other team members. It's something I'm aware of and actively work to balance."

This again gives the employer the opportunity to see what you might be like on the job as well as your perspective of both self-awareness and self-improvement.

Avoid Common Mistakes

There's no doubt that while getting the interview is very exciting, it is only one step in a longer process. Showing up to and delivering a great interview can help you stand out from the competition. Avoid some of these mistakes that are all too common in job interviews, so that when you stand out during these conversations, it's in a positive way.

Talking Too Long

An interviewer's time is precious, and you want to maximize the time offered. Taking six minutes to answer one question could leave the interviewer with brief opportunities to ask you other questions, so use your time wisely. Practice speaking in sound bites. These are around forty-five seconds to two minutes, which is enough time to present clear examples and make a point.

You want to provide an in-depth, detailed answer while giving the interviewer plenty of time to ask more questions. Most interviews will run from twenty-five to forty-five minutes, giving you ample time to answer several questions about yourself, and ask several of your own if you are concise.

Not Asking Your Own Questions

You are also vetting the employer to see if this is the right place for you to work. Many applicants spend most of their time preparing to answer questions about themselves and fail to prepare for the part of the interview where they get to ask their own questions.

Everyone should have at least two questions for their interviewer. You can prepare some in advance to glance at if you get stuck, but it's also good to pull on topics that were brought up by the interviewer. For example, maybe the interviewer briefly touched on the importance of company culture, but you want more details on how that shows up in the day to day.

This is not only appropriate to ask, but it shows you're serious about finding the right fit for you.

Not Doing Your Research

If the company has a podcast, listen to it. If they blog, read it. If they or the founders have published a book, read it. Most people don't do this or barely scratch the surface. If you can do this and then weave it into your interview in the form of explaining an example or relating it back to a question you have about what it's like to work there, all the better.

Doing your research beforehand also lets you skip past the basic questions and use your precious few minutes in the interview to ask more in-depth questions about an interest or concern that surfaced when you were researching the company, people, culture, or position. Don't waste that opportunity.

Assess During the Interview

During the interview, you want to look for a few specific things in addition to an overall feeling about whether or not you're excited about working with this company. Listen for:

▷ The way they talk about other employees

▷ How honest they are about the pros and cons of their team or processes

▷ Information about how often people from inside the company are promoted

▷ Details about team culture, commitment to employee wellness, and programs for professional development

▷ How the interviewer describes their own day to day. Do they sound excited? Exhausted? Overwhelmed?

Use these clues to determine whether this feels like the right fit for you in your professional journey. Never underestimate the impact of a gut feeling. If something feels off, it's worth trying to get a little more information to verify these concerns. Keep in mind, it may take more than one interview to get to the people you would be interacting with, so keep these assessments in mind throughout the process and compare your notes. Look for (in)consistency in answers.

End the Interview Well

Conclude the interview by telling the interviewer that you appreciated their time. As soon as possible after the interview, ideally within the hour, send a thank you note to the person who spoke to you. This can be sent over email and should highlight one memorable fact from your conversation.

Here's an example:

> Hi Mary,
> Thanks again for the opportunity to learn more about [ABC Company]. It was great to hear about the importance of excellent communication with the team—that's one of my top skill sets. I enjoyed getting to know you more and appreciate your time. I'm very interested in this position and look forward to [next steps discussed].

Connect with your interviewer on LinkedIn if you have not already, sending them a quick note about how much you enjoyed speaking with them.

If the interview went well, it should end with the interviewer telling you about the next steps in the process. If this doesn't happen naturally, feel free to bring it up so you have a time frame in mind. If they don't give you a clear date on which to follow up, check in ten to fourteen days later. If they've asked you not to follow up, don't send repeated emails.

Update your spreadsheet with your thoughts about how the interview went, any notes about requested follow up, or other information helpful for this job or a future interview.

Prepare for Post-Interview Assignments

Employers sometimes use test assignments to make sure the information shared in an application and interview matches a candidate's real skills. Usually, these are assignments only given to the top candidates, so it's a great sign when you are offered one. Test assignments are common for fields where an applicant can demonstrate their abilities in a short-term project, such as graphic design, writing, website development, or marketing. Employers should provide the assignment with clear instructions for completing it. If you aren't sure about any of the details, ask. It's better to clarify things upfront than miss getting the job because another applicant followed the instructions more closely.

Test assignments will usually be paid, have clear deadlines, and reflect some aspect of the job you will be doing if hired. The process gives employers a more concrete example of your skills in practice, and may give you as a candidate a better idea of how your skills will be applied to this job.

Accept Rejection

Getting an interview is certainly an indication that you're on the right path. Sadly, not all interviews lead to advancement in the process. Finding out that you didn't move forward to the next level of interviews or discovering that the company hired the other final candidate can be crushing. When that happens, remember this: You would not have been invited to interview if there wasn't something great about you that got this employer's attention.

Allow yourself to absorb the news when you get rejected, but always handle it professionally. Send a nice email in response thanking them for the information. It's okay to mention in this email that you're disappointed to hear this news. Keep your chin up and keep working on your application process, because the right job will come along.

It's appropriate at this point to share your concerns with a friend or a career coach. Sometimes, the timing isn't right or something else outside your control was at play, like promoting someone internally or another applicant being a little more qualified than you. Not every rejection is an indication that you did something wrong.

It does help, however, to talk things out and figure out if there were any places in the process where you could have done a better job, such as the interview or the test assignment. I once had to let a candidate know that we chose someone else because of the quality of the work submission. It was very hard to tell her that she hadn't been selected, and she immediately wanted to know what she could do better next time. This was a very professional way to handle disappointing news, and I'm sure my feedback helped her recalibrate and continue to improve her applications for similar positions.

The bottom line is this: It's okay to feel sad when you're rejected. But there is something worse than being rejected: not trying at all. The more doors you knock on, the bigger the chance that one of them is going to swing wide open for you.

Receive an Offer

The best-case scenario following your interview or a test assignment is an offer of employment. Although your excitement will be at peak levels during this time, remember that you do not have to accept an offer immediately. If this offer is extended to you over a video or phone call, let the company representative know that you are excited about this offer but would like some time to think things over. Give them a clear time frame when you will follow up, such as the next morning. No employer should bully you into accepting an offer outright or quickly over a call.

With a clear head, you can now step away from the hiring process and review your written and mental notes about the company and role to inform your response. There are a few ways to respond here:

> ▷ Accept the offer as presented to you by the employer and establish a start date.

> ▷ Decline the offer.

> ▷ Negotiate the offer.

Negotiating an Offer

Negotiation is an art form. If you feel like it's something that doesn't come naturally to you, make sure you take time to practice and learn more about how to negotiate effectively. These exercises can go a long way toward making you more comfortable in a negotiation situation if it comes up.

I found the process of negotiating on video to be quite nerve-wracking. When I originally applied for my last remote position, the pay range was not listed on the job description. At the conclusion of my first interview, the hiring manager reached out to let me know she believed I was overqualified for the job as listed, and she wanted to be honest about the company's original budget for the job. She shared that the company had received applications from more qualified people than expected, so she knew they might have to adjust their budget. When she stated the budget they had in mind, my heart sank. In that moment, I almost withdrew my name from consideration. I knew there was no way I could bring my all to a job with pay that was out of range with what I was expecting.

Frazzled, I turned to a military spouse friend of mine. I shared with her what the hiring manager had said and asked if I should just remove my name from the applicant list at this time. I'm so thankful she talked me out of it! Instead of saying "forget it," I wrote a clear and concise email that given the job duties we had talked about in the interview and my level of experience, I was hoping for a salary in a different range. What

I proposed was $25,000 higher than their stated budget. Not only did I get it, but they even upped it a little more in my formal offer letter. This is the power of negotiation.

When you're planning to negotiate an offer, use all the data you've collected so far in the application and interview process. Much of the equation has to do with the duties outlined in the position description or explained to you in the interview process. You can put yourself in the best possible position to negotiate if you can show that your skillset and experience are a notch above other candidates.

Negotiation is a two-way street. This means the employer can negotiate back or decline your offer altogether. Most employers offering salaried positions expect you to negotiate and will not be offended or caught off guard if you attempt it.

Compensation Negotiation

In order for negotiations to work, two things have to happen: the hiring manager has to want to hire you, and you have to make a good case for why you deserve more. Here are some tips for making this conversation less awkward and for truly owning your worth:

▷ Understand the person you're negotiating with. They will be the one to advocate for you. If this person is an HR rep, it is a win for them to get a great candidate who is excited about accepting an offer. Their perspective may be different from negotiating directly with your potential future supervisor. Set the tone that you'll be easy to work with but you have valid reasons for negotiating higher compensation.

▷ Being on the job market, you've already done your research and should have a good sense of market rates for someone with your expertise and experience. While this is a good starting point, don't say you want more money just because other companies are offering more. Review the comparable salaries of similar positions at other similar-sized companies in this company's geographic location. Other factors, such as revenue and expectations for the job also impact salary. In general, the bigger the company and the higher the revenue, the more opportunity there is to push for a bigger salary. You can still ask to be paid at least market rate for the role and your experience at a smaller company.

▷ Don't state that you just want a higher salary. Explain the justification for asking for more without sounding arrogant. If you can't come up with a good justification, reconsider asking for it.

▷ Reiterate your excitement to work for the company, if this is true. Consider this subtle but important distinction: employers want to know if you're trying to leverage your employment offer into higher offers from another company. If you can tell the company that you're very excited about this being the right place for you, this gives them more peace of mind that an adjusted offer might get them the "yes" they are hoping for.

Negotiating Options Beyond Salary

While pay is the most common line item you may negotiate in an employment offer, it is not your only room for leverage. There are many other things you can negotiate into your contract depending on the employer and the specifics of the offer. Here are some examples:

▷ More vacation time

▷ More flexible hours

▷ Not traveling as much, if the position requires it

▷ Childcare allowance

▷ Reimbursement of your home work expenses, such as internet or cell phone costs

▷ A gym allowance (especially if the company does offer an onsite gym for those who work in their physical office)

▷ Other incentives like bonuses or extra paid sick time

In some cases, especially if you're fully covered for health insurance as a military spouse, you may be able to suggest alternatives to health coverage to increase your paycheck.

If you want to negotiate multiple things at once, do them together. Don't make the hiring manager run back and forth with your requests. If you are asking for multiple things together, such as a higher salary, flex time, and a later start date, clearly indicate which are most important to you.

While this is most applicable to employment situations, independent contractors also have room to negotiate. Keep in mind a company—or you—may have restrictions on what can be offered due to your independent contractor status. Aspects that make the process more efficient or practical for either of you are good terms to consider as well as payment schedules that help your cash flow to cover project expenses. For example, prepayment terms for upfront project supplies, different rates for specialized services, or payments at select milestones.

Whether you haven't gotten your dream offer yet or just read through this to prepare for an upcoming negotiation, stick with it! The employment search is hard, but the more prepared and confident you are, the easier it is to navigate.

Chapter 7

Grow Your Career

Congratulations—you got the job! After a lot of hard work, you're here. This is not the end of your journey though—this is a new beginning. Whether you hope to stay at this company long-term, move into another industry at some point, or get hired by another company in a similar position, this is a good time to set up a plan to help you achieve that.

Adjust to Your New Role

Whether your new job is similar to a previous position or completely different, there will be an adjustment period. When it comes to processes, communication standards, and even inside jokes, some things must be learned on the job and it's not always easy.

The first days of any new position involve the sharing of a lot of information and an adjustment to working with a new team in a new role and possibly for the first time in a remote environment. Give yourself grace and the opportunity to adapt. You may have set big goals after receiving a very competitive offer from the company, which makes you want to hit the ground running and achieve as much as possible to show you were the right choice. It will take time to adapt though, and your first several weeks will likely involve plenty of meetings, company policy reviews, video trainings, and other onboarding activities—in addition to doing your work. This is not lost time as it will make it much easier for you to do your job within this company.

You may have a designated probationary period, typically three to six months, in which your employer will evaluate your job performance and decide whether or not you will remain at the company. Other companies may include an "at will" clause in their employment agreement, meaning you can be let go (or leave) at any time without cause. The details of this should have been discussed with you by the time you accept an offer but, in any case, your new employer will see you with a critical eye during the initial few weeks. Getting a few small wins and forming relationships with your new coworkers goes a long way toward showing you are a great addition to the team. During the first few months of your new role, your company may also have formal or informal onboarding procedures.

Onboarding

This company hired you because they believe you will make a great contribution to their team and goals. They also know it may take time for you to feel confident in your role and to master essential tasks, software, and procedures.

Onboarding is a chance for you to ask questions, learn the nuances of your new role, figure out how your work interacts with and impacts others, and inevitably, make some mistakes that will help you learn and grow. Keep an evolving document of your questions so you can work through them as you perform your work and develop relationships with your supervisor and colleagues.

Following a few best practices will help ensure an effective onboarding experience.

Read Company Materials

First of all, read the company handbook, watch any training videos, and get a clear understanding of employer policies and procedures. You will likely receive this type of information after you've signed new-employee paperwork, before or on your first day. It's tempting to skim through these materials, but it is well worth making sure you understand every aspect of your new position and your new company. You will also likely generate questions based on your review of these materials, so add those to your running questions document.

Connect With Colleagues

Early in your onboarding process, establish yourself as part of the team. It is up to you to proactively develop working relationships with your new colleagues, especially in a remote environment. Schedule time to speak with each individual to better understand their role, their perspective on the company, and who they are as a person. Set up coffee chats or virtual lunches. It might also help you to plan some small talk topics to use when you're introduced to these new colleagues.

Avoid getting involved in any unnecessary drama or office politics, especially those that pre-date your arrival. You can form authentic relationships with coworkers while steering clear of office gossip. Remain neutral and try to disengage with anyone who wants to continue that type of conversation. Embrace the positives of your new workplace culture as much as possible.

You and your colleagues will also be learning how to best work together as you begin to integrate into the company and execute your responsibilities. Be aware of the situation you are entering and its impact on the team. Are you joining a high-performing remote team and your role is a new one due to growing success? Or is your role filling a long-open gap on an overworked team? If this hiring has been long overdue, you may need to balance between completing enough work to relieve pressure of other team members, while not setting a precedent that you will always handle such a high volume.

Match Expectations With Your Supervisor

As early as possible, arrange a comprehensive meeting with your supervisor to clarify their perspective of your role and how it connects to the company's bigger values, mission, and goals. This might be the first meeting with your new supervisor as you step into your remote role. Plan another one a couple of weeks later to ask questions and address any open concerns at that point in time.

Be as methodical as possible when executing your new responsibilities. If your supervisor or team members expect a lot from you, it's easy to want to jump in and get to work quickly or to manage your day to please others. Instead, make sure you get a clear understanding of how operations work at this company. Take time to prioritize based on your deliverables.

Evaluate Your Role

Another thing to watch for early on is whether or not the tasks, expectations, and schedule of the job match up with how they were explained to you in the job description and hiring process. If changes have evolved, such as your employer trusting you with more responsibility or asking you to take on different tasks than those outlined in the job description, you may need to revisit and update this with your supervisor.

Depending on the situation, this might also prompt you to have a conversation around adjusting your pay. In some cases, an employer will see that you work faster, more diligently, or at a very high level and throw more opportunities your way.

However, if you're finding the additional duties or opportunities are not in line with the position you accepted, it is perfectly reasonable to raise concerns or turn down some of the opportunities extended your way. The offer for you to learn new things, take on new roles, or manage other team members shows a great deal of confidence in you. Making sure your job description accurately reflects your actual responsibilities will help ensure you are compensated and evaluated fairly.

Track Your Contributions

Right from the beginning, document your contributions. Create your own personal roadmap that covers your first three months in this new position. Doing this will help you reflect back at your first quarterly or semi-annual evaluation. Not only will you be able to easily summarize what you've been able to achieve since joining the team, this is also a way of holding yourself accountable. Note challenges you have faced, how you overcame them, and major contributions to the team. Continue to meet with your supervisor at regular intervals to review and make necessary course corrections. More frequent check-ins with your direct supervisor can also clue you in to steps you need to take to advance in your role.

If promotion opportunities do exist after a few months on the job, have a candid conversation with your supervisor or human resources manager about what you would need to do, exemplify, and accomplish to be considered for a promotion. Many employers appreciate this direct approach, and this will give you a great window into what they perceive as a gap between where you are now and where you want to go. You can use this information to develop yourself professionally and continue contributing to the team. Documenting this information is also helpful down the road if you need to approach salary negotiations again.

Make sure you know the company's policy on performance reviews and what you can expect once you've finished your onboarding process or probationary period.

Discover the Bigger Picture

Much of the early onboarding process is about connecting to the role at hand, getting access to important accounts, and learning the basic culture of the company. This process takes time and should not be rushed; it will be easier for you to grow in your role when you approach this with care.

Over time, you'll want to learn more about the company beyond your role. Working remotely can sometimes feel like you are disconnected from the bigger picture, especially if some colleagues see each other in the physical office on a regular basis. Learning more about the mission and vision of your company and how your contributions impact or shape the larger goals can inspire your daily work. It can also set you up for promotions, advancements, raises, and other ways to grow within your individual role and the company at large.

Be an observer. Before you start bringing ideas to the table, discover how your role and department fit into the larger organization. Take note of existing dynamics and how choices are evaluated and decisions made. Read company reports and pay attention to information released to the press or investors. See your work from many different perspectives.

Find a Mentor

You can learn a lot from colleagues who have more experience in the industry as well as more experience with this particular company. As you become more integrated into the company, seek authentic connections with leaders and prospective mentors you respect who can help you genuinely contribute and grow. Take advantage of work-related ways to speak with them and make a good impression. Don't be over-eager to share how great you are and all you achieved in your first few months. If there's a leader you respect, observe how they interact with other leaders. Show up to team meetings with clear questions, intelligent suggestions, or an extra willingness to step into new projects to show your initiative.

Here are a few ways to do this naturally:

▷ Once you're more comfortable in your role, seek to join committees or task forces on the job where you can make a real contribution.

▷ Listen to your coworkers and leaders. What obstacles are blocking success both at the individual and team level? Are you a problem solver who can propose unique solutions?

▷ Show up to presentations made by company leaders you respect, both within the company or at conferences, and take thoughtful notes about their perspectives. Ask interesting follow-up questions.

▷ Ask your supervisor what they think is the company's biggest challenge. Consider how you might be able to proactively create initiatives or programs that aim to solve or alleviate that problem.

▷ Find ways for the company to improve its public image or contribute to a better life for employees. Ideas could range from diversity and inclusion programs, to environmental efforts to reduce the company's waste, or a leadership training program.

▷ Once you've made a positive impression with some of the above efforts, ask your intended mentor to coffee. Have a clear ask for them of what a mentorship would look like. Perhaps that's a monthly thirty-minute meeting where you ask them structured questions, or a roundtable event every other month with you and a few other employees who also want to benefit from this leader's expertise. Clearly indicate what you hope to gain from the mentorship, why you chose them, and how respectful you'll be of their time.

Mentors can fast track your professional development and inspire you on a regular basis. If your company doesn't have a formal mentorship program, you could use what you learn from your own experience to create one.

Create a Professional Development Plan

A professional development plan is used to document your career goals and define the strategy through which you will attempt to achieve them. It takes planning and time to create a good plan, but this is an excellent way to ensure you meet your own professional goals and achieve career milestones.

Remember that professional development is your own responsibility. Your employer might have shared information with you about professional development benefits when you were hired, such as reimbursements for certifications, online trainings, and other learning materials. You may be expected to create a professional development plan related to your job as part of a performance review process. A personal professional development plan, however, can help you achieve your long-term career goals beyond this position or company.

Start your professional development plan by documenting your current career progress. You already did much of this work as part of the application process but look back over the past year, three years, or five years, and determine what you have done specifically in that time period to contribute to your own professional development. Then answer the question, "Am I where I thought I'd be at this stage in my career?"

A professional development plan is a great opportunity to correct situations in which you have not actively been involved in professional development on your own or cases in which you answered this question above with a no. Reflect on your actions and then identify any other factors that have hindered or helped your professional development.

Now that you know your starting place, identify your specific career goals. Where do you want to be a year or three years from now? What additional skills, licenses, or experiences do you need to get there? Consider questions like:

- Am I seeing a version of my future success in my current position?

- What activities about my job do I love the most?

- What does success mean to me?

- What are the tools, technical skills, or software I would like to learn in the next year to become more competent at my job and in this industry overall?

- What soft skills could I improve to be more effective?

The next step is to decide on a strategy that is realistic, embedded in your position, and ongoing. Consider all the types of development available to you and how you learn best. Your plan might include books, podcasts, university courses, technical skills training, management retreats, professional certifications, interpersonal skills practice, research, volunteer roles, participation in professional organizations, and more.

Create a timeline of when you want to achieve your development goals; this is critical for sticking to your plan. Giving yourself a deadline increases your chances of success. At a maximum, set targets on a yearly basis. Many people find six-week sprints or ninety-day sprints effective in breaking down bigger goals. Continue to update your plan as you go along and readjust goals if you miss them and need to recalibrate.

Upskilling

Taking your professional development upon yourself is an important step in growing both as a person and in your professional career. There are also other tools you can use to level-up your soft skills, hard skills, or new skills that emerge as a result of technology. This is known in most cases as upskilling and reskilling and, similar to other professional development, can be accomplished by taking online courses, following podcasts, reading books, and partnering with mentors.

One of the biggest reasons to engage in upskilling and reskilling as it relates to your job is because the rapid evolution of digital technology has significant implications, especially in remote or virtual roles. Upskilling positions you to adapt and pivot as needed. Because automation threatens many existing jobs, upskilling is crucial for you to protect yourself against changes in your industry or in the company that you might not anticipate. While many of the skills you may wish to pursue aren't considered high-tech skills, doing consistent research to determine what will most contribute to your overall knowledge can help you identify how to remain a top talent amid rapid changes.

Reskilling refers to short-term initiatives undertaken for certain groups. An upskilling effort, however, is a comprehensive initiative to convert your existing knowledge into productive results or adapting to new technology. Your employer will value you for this as they are thinking about ways to mitigate risks in their own company. This also positions you well to continue growing within the company or, if needed, to leverage future job opportunities.

Here are a few easy ways to stay up to date on skills:

▷ Set Google alerts for your industry, with the words "trends" or "studies" following it.

▷ Follow media sources in your field.

▷   Read new books on leadership, management, tech, and your industry.

▷   Attend industry conferences, workshops, or webinars.

▷   Network with experts in the field on LinkedIn.

Online courses are a great resource for training and certifications. Sites like Udemy.com are a great place to find affordable online courses in your field and to learn new things. Other places to find online courses include Coursera, Skillshare, and Lynda training on LinkedIn.

The Institute for Veteran and Military Families (IVMF) also offers industry-specific certification training for free to qualified military spouses. This includes recognized and valued certifications like Google IT Support Professional, Systems Security Certified Practitioner, Agile Certified Practitioner, Project Management Professional, Six Sigma Green Belt, and many more. Military spouses and veterans are entitled to one free course and industry exam payment through IVMF, and these programs can be completed online.

Prepare for Regular Employee Reviews

Every company approaches the employee review process differently, but you should anticipate at least an informal quarterly review with your direct supervisor. When you are onboarding into the company, ask for details about how reviews will be conducted. Will the employer go through specific tasks, reports, or questions during this time? What should you be prepared to discuss? Who provides input to your performance evaluation?

Some companies use a 360-degree review, which means supervisors, direct reports, and team members all evaluate each other. You may have a mixture of informal reviews and formal reviews with written feedback forms.

Beginning to prepare for reviews during your onboarding will help you feel more confident as these conversations emerge. The first review is definitely the most nerve-wracking, but having a clear understanding of what this process looks like at the company will help you tremendously.

Don't count on your supervisor to remember how long you've been in your position or to keep a running tab of all the things you've learned or accomplished during this period. You should keep track of your own highlights, map your progress against your objectives and job description, and review your own professional development plan before the meeting so your key points are top of mind.

Reevaluate Questionable Fit

It is very hard to acknowledge when a job or a company is not the right fit for you. This does not mean there is something wrong with you or that you have failed at your position. Instead, it shows a high level of self-awareness that you know when you're not at your best.

First, give the position and the company your best effort. Things can easily be misinterpreted in a remote work environment, so allow for a month of adjusting to your new role and team. If you spot behavior that develops into ongoing patterns, however, and you have not been able to directly influence a change or there's no interest from company leaders to correct it, start thinking about the extent of this problem for you.

No one deserves to stay in a toxic work environment. If you're feeling overwhelmed, disconnected, annoyed, or angry about your job on a daily basis, this can affect every aspect of your life and likely isn't contributing to the company well, either. If you've made a genuine effort to try to fit in and the company culture is not a fit or you're subjected to something outside your control that has drastically altered the working arrangement, you might need to consider resigning.

Imagine, for example, that you had a great experience with the hiring manager during the interview stage, and this person was introduced to you as the person who would be your manager in this role. If that person were to be promoted or transferred after your interview and you now are working under someone with whom you don't communicate well or a person who has a completely different approach to work, your dreams of a great remote job could turn into nightmares instead. In these cases, it's best to be honest both with yourself and the company. Set a timeline for getting back out onto the job market and set a goal deadline for when you'll exit this role.

While it might be tempting to burn bridges on your way out, avoid this if at all possible. There's usually little to be gained from doing this. If you're leaving a truly toxic work environment, it's unlikely any troublemakers in question will adjust their behavior just because of a loud exit from you.

Be honest with your boss and tell them you don't think this is working out well for either party. Give them plenty of notice so they have time to hire someone else. Exit professionally and continue searching for a job that's a better fit for you if you haven't yet obtained one.

If you do need to depart from the role or company, consider if there are any lessons or clues you need to watch for as you go back into the job-hunting process.

When is a Role Toxic?

Many people desire a career that supports both their personal and professional goals in life. In the past, plenty of people, including military spouses who might have felt they were at a disadvantage, might have stayed in a position longer simply because they wanted the tenure on their resume or the income from their pay. However, remote work has opened so many opportunities and more workers than ever are considering when toxicity overrides the benefits of working remotely.

The definition of a toxic workplace is evolving, too. In the past, people might have referred to illegal activity or true abuse or harassment as the basic definition of a toxic workplace. With employees having more choices than ever and some employers struggling to fill roles, culture takes a front and center spot as something to think about in your daily work life.

No job is worth your mental health. If you find that you have made attempts to resolve toxic issues and you've been ignored or gaslit in the process, it might be time to start looking for a new job.

Subtle toxicity can occur remotely and negatively impact your life. This can appear in things like:

> A culture of overwork, where people show up early, work late, work weekends, or expect to receive responses outside established working hours

> Team members who do not support your work or have unrealistic expectations

> Supervisors who want to use screencapture software or check in constantly to prove you are working

> Leaders who won't listen to you when you report that something is off at work

> Lack of inclusive policies or practices that show a lack of concern about equity, diversity, and inclusion

These are just a few examples of how issues can add up to feel like a toxic workplace. What reads as unbearable for you might be different. In one past role, I raised concerns reported to me by multiple employees. Management ignored the concerns and insisted the problem was with the employees in question, so I chose to resign from that remote position. While working in an in-person office can certainly amplify issues of toxicity, that doesn't mean remote work eliminates those same toxic concerns.

Company leaders should care about their employees and their contractors enough to provide a safe and enjoyable place to work. If you start to notice red flags, trust your gut. Bring up issues as honestly and nonconfrontationally as possible and give the employer an opportunity to respond. If your concerns are ignored or downplayed, file this away as a serious red flag that might start you back on the job search path.

Chapter 8 —

Honor Balance and Ethics

F inding and getting your dream remote job is only the first part of the journey. Once you begin working in a position, you will focus on integrating into your new company and determining your professional growth plan for this role and your career. Working remotely also brings unique challenges, even after you are comfortable in a position or have worked multiple remote jobs. In this chapter, we will discuss how to prepare for and address some of these challenges before you start working remotely and after you are on the job.

Whether you stay in this remote position for years or pivot at some point in the future, the tips in this chapter will help you thrive in remote employment as well as consider some of the key ethical decisions related to working from home.

Plan for Work-at-Home Challenges

Working from home has many advantages for contractors and employees who find that it suits their environment and personality, but there are also some downsides. Proactively planning for the challenges can reduce their impact when you start a new position or move to a new military duty station and set up your next home office.

Manage Workload

For many years, some employers avoided offering remote work because of the perception that people aren't as focused and couldn't be trusted to work on their own. But actually, many remote employees work more than necessary. Whether intended to overcompensate for an employer's concerns about possible distractions and reduced productivity, or to overcommunicate in an effort to show the employer they are online all the time, overworking is unnecessary and unhealthy.

Balancing at-home workload is a common concern for military spouses. Grateful to be in the role, some have genuine concerns about their coworkers' perception of their ability to focus when outside factors affect their personal life—such as deployment or a long-term separation from a spouse living in a different state. Know that you are not required to overwork and that the right company will support you in your daily role without micromanaging you.

If you've had an honest conversation with your employer about their remote work expectations, you should already know how you can most effectively communicate with your supervisor and the rest of the team. If your employer does bring up concerns about you being distracted, don't take it personally. Plenty of other people face personal challenges, such as caring for a loved one or personal health issues, moving to new homes, or experiencing some other kind of disorganization that impacts their ability to be productive. If your employer is fair in their assessment that you are going through things on a personal front that are truly impacting your productivity, then work with them to come up with a plan.

That said, it is easy to fall into the habit of overworking, especially if this is your first remote position or if you convinced your former employer to let you work remotely. Here are some tips to help you keep an appropriate work schedule:

> ▷ Use a time tracker to see how much time you are really working each day.

> ▷ Resist the temptation to check in early or to look at email or messaging systems after hours.

> ▷ Take an honest lunch break and block it off on your calendar so it doesn't get filled up with a meeting that leaves you no breaks.

> ▷ Set reminders on your phone to get up and take stretch breaks, take the dog on a walk, or step away from your computer.

> ▷ Use a go-to-work and end-of-workday set of rituals to mark these transitions in your life.

Communicate Clearly

Remote teams do have to focus on communication more than many in-person teams for several reasons. First, it's easy to become so focused on your own tasks that you mentally check out of what the company as a whole is doing. Second, much of remote communication relies on text, email, or instant messages, which can easily be misinterpreted or misconstrued. Third, remote teams don't have the benefit of getting to see someone's day-to-day experience at work, where you can pick up important clues by reading someone's body language. When you see a team member for a short time on a video call, it's hard to tell if something in their personal life or work life is really affecting them unless it's brought up by you or them. Finally, as previously mentioned, sometimes team members overcommunicate to try to prove they are working.

While some of these communication efforts have good intentions, it becomes distracting for the entire team when there are constant emails, phone calls, messages, or notifications popping up. Does the sales team really need to be notified about an operations team update? If not, don't copy them on the email or in a general thread. Communicate clearly, effectively, and as needed with the right people.

As a worker, you are sensitive to (in)effective communication with coworkers, so use these moments for self-awareness: What is your communication style? Do you tend to over or under communicate? Do you pick up the phone to more effectively talk through issues and reduce misunderstandings? As you find your footing in a position and feel more comfortable sharing ideas and strategies with others, you might mention trends you've spotted in over or under communication and suggest improvements.

Much like overworking, military spouses tend to feel pressure to communicate that they are indeed working and focused on the job or to report in too often with updates. Get a feel for the company's general approach to communication and don't feel you need to go above and beyond. Focus on being clear, punctual, respectful, and professional.

Take Breaks

At home, where there are arguably plenty of distractions or easy access to the snack pantry, your first instinct might be that you'll be able to take plenty more breaks. One thing I discovered in making the transition to remote work is that it's not always easy for other members of the team to realize how many hours you might spend sitting in your chair on a given workday. Meetings can easily get booked back-to-back. By the time you finally do get out of one meeting, you might feel pressure to check your email or respond to that one message that's been in the back of your mind all day.

Working remotely, you've got to be able to prioritize and take charge of your own breaks. For me, this meant physically putting them in my calendar so they couldn't turn into meetings from a well-meaning coworker who saw open space in my schedule. I also set phone alarms to remind me to get up, walk around, step outside, and drink a glass of water. One of the biggest things that helped was scheduling an actual lunch break and not allowing myself to eat lunch at my computer. Step into a different room to take your lunch break. You need that actual break in order to decompress and come back to the work at hand refreshed.

Working from home, especially in front of a screen all day, is not good for your health if you don't take breaks. If you average more than an hour in front of a screen, get yourself a pair of blue light glasses to wear. These have many powerful benefits, including less eye strain and fewer headaches. Too much blue light also makes it hard for many people to fall asleep, so you might even see benefits after work hours if you wear your glasses all day.

As a get-ready-to-work-remotely exercise, brainstorm ten things you could do to take a break from your work, step away from screens, and get moving. Some examples might include:

- ▷ Stretch

- ▷ Meditate

- ▷ Eat a healthy snack and drink a glass of water

- ▷ Take the dog for a quick walk

- ▷ Listen to music or ten minutes of an audio book

- ▷ Mini-exercise, such as a set of jumping jacks

Engage With People

Talking to people online all day is not the same thing as in-person interaction. Having to save up questions, concerns, or celebrations for specific meeting times requires intention, and sharing those does not always inspire the same sense of collaboration as it might if you were in person and could hop over to a coworker's cubicle.

Many remote employees face a risk of isolation, a fact that can be amplified for military spouses whose networks of friends and family members might be spread all over the world. Adapting to a new duty station can be hard for spouses to begin with, but add in working remotely, and this requires much more planning to remain connected to others.

Create a list of activities that help you feel connected to other people. This could be getting together in person, meeting for coffee, walking together on your lunch break, texting, calling, emailing, or even writing letters to other people. It could be participating in networking groups near your base or in online communities for professionals in your industry. Think about how these could be incorporated into your work life or your personal life on a regular basis.

Know yourself when it comes to isolation risk. Some people are comfortable with remote work right away, only needing to connect with coworkers when necessary in meetings. Others crave a coffee or watercooler chat like they may get in an office. If this is important to you, remember to ask about it during the hiring process to get a general sense of how the company supports connection.

One simple tip that goes a long way in building relationships with other people, including customers or clients of the company you work with, is to seek out personal connection, even if it's just for a few minutes at the beginning of a video or phone meeting. This is critical if you are in an executive or managerial role.

Get to know people's hobbies, likes, dislikes, and their families. If you only connect with a certain coworker once a week, spend the first three minutes seeing how they are doing. Are they celebrating an exciting milestone you could acknowledge? Are they dealing with family illness or other stressors that may be impacting their work? Do you need to gently encourage them to take time off for themselves? Showing empathy and interest in other people brings some of the human aspect into remote work, and it's powerful for building connections and becoming a better employee yourself. It only takes a few minutes to connect with someone, but it helps both of you consider this personal aspect.

Set Office Boundaries

Working remotely does not mean friends, family, or neighbors can interrupt you whenever they want or take advantage of your flexible schedule. Set your work boundaries in time and space so it's clear to everyone when you are at work.

You might have a dedicated room in your home where you work. Or perhaps a corner of your kitchen or a repurposed closet serves as your remote office. If you don't have a home office to yourself with a door that closes, share this information with your employer to verify that what you do have in your home will work. Together you might find alternatives, such as a coworking space in your community.

When you have a home office with a door that closes and a space to call your own, it allows you to focus on work when you are in your working hours, and more easily remind your family not to disturb you when your door is closed.

At the end of your work day, leave your work space. Close the door to your home office for the evening. If that's in your kitchen, invest in a set of portable crates, file organizers, or a rolling desk to easily close up your work and put it out of sight. This sets a boundary for you to transition to personal time.

Beyond best practices for yourself, be aware of how your role and everything you do impacts and is governed by the ethics and values of your company.

Ethics of Working Remotely

Once you're hired, you'll want to check with your employer about any specific policies regarding how you work. Independent contractors are largely in charge of their own work parameters, but employees take direction from their employer.

While you might think you have a clear concept of what working remotely means for you, everyone has to be on the same page. Companies with remote employees should have a remote work policy documented where all members of the team can easily find it. Companies that are new to remote hiring may not have official policies yet. If yours does not have a documented plan, adopt best practices to help you stay on track and build a relationship of credibility and trust with your employer. Clarity around expectations makes it easier to follow policies and meet expectations confidently. Determine:

▷ Expectations around general working hours

▷ What home offices are expected to include, such as if they must have a door that closes

▷ Allowed schedule flexibility, such as going out for lunch or to a dentist appointment. Do you have to tell your supervisor? Can you make up that hour from your appointment later or do you need to take paid time off?

▷ What meetings each team member is expected to attend on a weekly or monthly basis

These and similar topics may also be included in an employee handbook under a code of conduct policy that specifies expected ethical behaviors in the workplace. At a minimum, this usually includes obeying all company policies, professionalism and respect for colleagues, and safeguarding company property. Remote work policies follow these rules with additional considerations for off-site locations. Be intentional about your approach.

Draw a Line Between Professional and Personal

If you can't already tell, being intentional with your work area, work time, and work focus are recurring themes that will help make you more successful. Many of the same considerations for working from home effectively have ethical components. The first of these is to clearly distinguish between your work at home and your life at home. The ethical component resides in gray areas of that boundary.

No matter how much you love your work and no matter how honest and disciplined you are, you will have a morning when you are super tired from not sleeping well. Or a day when your personal to-do list is really long (and laundry piled high), while your work projects or meeting schedules are light. You may be tempted to blend days like those to take advantage of your "invisible" remoteness. Have a plan to address those situations, honoring the policies and agreements of your role.

Some work-from-home employees also have a side business or hobby they do after work hours. Most independent contractors have multiple clients, some of which have specific confidentiality and security requirements. Depending on your situation, the boundary you need to make might be between your multiple work personas. For example, you might need a different section of your office for different equipment or files, separate email addresses and software licenses, and distinctly separate work schedules.

Even if you have only one remote work position, it is important to keep any company-supplied equipment and company information separate from your personal devices and files. A good way to think about this separation is to imagine that within the hour you will need to give your manager all of your work-related equipment, software, passwords, and work files. Could you easily do that and have no concerns about personal information on your work computer or work files on your personal devices? If you are an independent contractor or an employee whose company doesn't provide you a separate computer, use a different browser to keep work and personal searches separate. Back up files onto different work and personal cloud accounts or separate external drives.

The extent of your professional-personal boundaries will in part be determined by who supplies your equipment.

Equipment

Generally, independent contractors provide their own equipment unless specific tools are necessary for the project and agreed upon ahead of time. If a client does supply you with equipment, software licenses, or other tools, be sure to use them only for that client that paid for or supplied them.

As an employee, it is reasonable to expect equipment to be provided to you. As early as the first interview for a remote position, you can ask for further details about the company's remote equipment policy. At a minimum, you should acquire the tools you need to accomplish regular work tasks, such as:

- A computer and separate monitor
- A separate keyboard and mouse
- A good set of headphones or earbuds
- An internet connection that is reliable and fast enough to support video calls or any other heavy bandwidth aspects of your position

Optional equipment includes:

- A convertible desk that allows you to sit or stand

▷ A microphone (recommended if you are on meetings often or involved in recording videos or podcasts)

▷ Separate phone/number if you will receive calls from your company's customers or clients

▷ Specialized software or tools needed for your work

Any equipment supplied by the company you work for should be used only and specifically for doing work for that company. Don't cross-purpose company equipment for a side business or your personal life.

Understand clearly what your responsibility is regarding equipment updates and maintenance, accidental damage, on-site repairs, parts replacement, IT support or troubleshooting, and so on. Some of this will be normal course of business similar to if you were working in an office, but remote work has its own challenges. A toddler, pet, or bouncing ball could make its way to a laptop screen despite your best efforts. For military spouses transitioning a remote role from one duty station to another, you'll also need to consider liability during the move.

Checking In and Checking Out

As previously mentioned, setting rituals to formally signal you are starting or ending your workday helps you manage your own productivity and work-life balance. It also helps you honor your agreed upon work hours.

Your colleagues working in a position outside their home have visible, tangible transition points, such as a commute, walking into a building, or booting up an in-office computer to signal officially checking in to work. They may also have a badge or timecard or other official log in.

If you are not required to officially log in and out, be intentional about how you will hold yourself accountable. Set timer reminders on your phone or use a time tracker app. From a productivity and personal transition perspective, you can match this with other habits that help you check in to work, such as drinking a cup of coffee. From an ethical perspective, maintaining more formality to your routine respects your time commitment, especially on days when competing demands require you to stretch your flexibility.

Physical location also falls under this area. For example, if you want to work from a coffee shop some mornings, you'll want to verify if it is acceptable. Most companies don't consider public spaces the same type of remote workspace as a quiet, dedicated home office. The same might go for having another family member use your office during typical work hours. This may create distractions or sound issues when you are in meetings, or could present security or confidentiality concerns.

Security

Your employer might have specific rules or best practices around security, so you should ask this in your onboarding and read through any employee handbook to make sure you are aware of potential issues with your computer. Most frequently, the security concerns relate to your internet connection, file storage, and passwords. If you are required to download or use specific programs to meet security requirements for your employer, verify that you have done this before starting work.

Even if your new workplace does not mandate certain security requirements, it's smart to protect your data and theirs. Here are a few easy ways to do that:

> ▷ Use an encryption tool if you work from different locations, homes, or travel often for work. Think twice before connecting to any public WiFi without using encryption. This not only protects your work, but also any information about your company, its intellectual property, or its clients that resides on or is connected to your computer.

▷ Use a secure password manager and a variety of strong passwords. Do not repeat passwords among accounts as a breach of one may create greater risk of exposure for another.

▷ Don't allow friends or family to use your work computer.

▷ Don't open unexpected attachments or emails that might be phishing attempts.

▷ Respect your service member's security clearance and other related requirements when it comes to sharing information about them with your new coworkers.

Self-Awareness

Evaluating your own work ethic requires you to be self-aware and willing to learn and improve. In the resume and interview sections of this book, you learned about putting your best foot forward when it comes to showcasing your ability to work remotely. The work doesn't end there. You will discover your own challenges working remotely, and you will need to remain open to better ways of doing things.

Self-awareness and a good team go a long way. Rely on your manager or team members to help when you encounter challenges. If you notice your own bad habits emerging or challenges you didn't expect popping up in ways that affect your work, be ready to share these openly and honestly. If a coworker has more experience than you do working remotely, they could recommend resources or strategies.

Once the excitement of a new role fades, be aware of issues that shift your mindset or outcomes in the months following. Identify what you do and don't like about your role or working from home. Brainstorm if there are ways to change that or if a call with your supervisor about responsibilities is on the to do list. Review your job description regularly and match it up against the work you are doing, since this can help illustrate when you are doing things you weren't hired to do. This can also help make the case for promotions and raises.

Time Off

Treat your remote role the same as an in-office role when you are sick. If your body needs time to rest, or if you are not mentally focused on work because you are feeling poorly, you need to take sick time. For a remote worker, this means not working from home. It may seem like jumping on a video call is no big deal, but you can't bring your best self to your workday when you're not well, so step back and respect your need to recuperate. Follow the company's procedure to notify your supervisor and then disconnect for the day or half day.

The same ethics apply when taking time out of the office for vacation. Follow the company's policy about how much notice to give, the official process for requesting or noting that time off so other team members are aware. Provide reminders to any direct reports a few days in advance, and set an out-of-office message on your email and voicemail, noting a backup in case someone needs an immediate response.

Ethics of Exiting

There are as many reasons for exiting a position as there are for accepting one. Perhaps you received a better job offer. Maybe your career interests have changed, or you obtained a new credential that qualifies you for other opportunities.

Sometimes, through no fault of your own, the role or the company is just not a fit for you. This can be frustrating, especially if you spent a lot of time trying to find the right position and asked all the right questions during the application process. All jobs have this potential for reality to be different from initial perceptions.

Maybe you are only considering leaving and you want to prepare yourself for the possibility. Your doubts may stem from mismatches between stated company values or processes and the words and actions of company leaders. If toxic behaviors have emerged or the position is very different from how it was advertised, remember that you likely won't be doing your best work if you stay in a role that's not for you. If this is the case, begin planning your process for how and when you'll leave.

Don't stay in a role you are unhappy with just because it's remote. Poor leadership, overwork, unreasonable demands, bad communication, harassment, and other related issues can take place in remote work, too.

It's also possible the reason for your exit is that you are being let go. If this is the case, get as much information as you can about the reason for your termination so you can use any lessons learned in your next position. An employer is usually not obligated to give you a reason, but termination due to performance should never be a surprise to you. Good managers will have brought up any performance-related concerns in your early reviews, along with corrective actions or development plans. The situation may not have anything to do with your performance; it could be due to budget constraints after lost revenue, restructuring after a merger or divestiture, or one of many other scenarios.

Regardless of the reason for leaving your position, make your exit as professional and smooth as possible for everyone involved. Give your notice, follow termination/resignation procedures, and honor your final responsibilities and commitments. Be an outstanding, ethical employee through the end.

All previous best practices apply. Don't fall into the temptation of using your remote status to job search during work hours. Don't speak poorly of the company or coworkers. Be prompt in returning any equipment and carefully follow procedures for transitioning company information. Understand when you will lose access to your email account and files, and know the rules about what you can do or say to communicate your departure to colleagues or clients. Reread your contract for any noncompete clauses, confidentiality timelines, and other legal restrictions you may have for other positions within the field or with competitor companies.

Independent contractors usually have a cleaner exit since many of the employee transitions don't apply, but it is just as important to manage a professional departure. If you enjoyed working with this company and hope to gain contracts in the future, you want to express that to your primary contact. That person may have other projects or may move to another position within the company or to a different company. They will remember your closure on this project. If your experience with this company was not positive, it is still valuable and essential to your contractor status and business to maintain your positive reputation as a professional throughout the contracting process. Keep the good in your goodbye.

Remote Work Journey

After working a remote position, you may decide to pursue this environment throughout your career, especially as you continue to move with the military. Or you may incorporate aspects of remote work into a hybrid office-virtual position. It's possible you will hold more than one remote position or work with more than one company before you find a great fit. Remote work is a journey, and as you grow and evolve, your career will too. Embrace the learning opportunity and continue to check in with yourself on a monthly or quarterly basis. As with any in-office position, a specific remote or hybrid position may fulfill a purpose for a period of time in your career, or may give you valuable experience for other opportunities. The good news is that as more companies embrace the benefits of remote work, your pool of potential employers gets bigger.

There are so many benefits—and challenges—to working remotely. Here are some of my favorite tips that have helped me in my remote work journey:

- ▷ Invest in a home-office environment that promotes your wellness.
  - ✓ Consider a convertible standing/sitting desk and get an anti-fatigue floor mat if you switch to standing at least part of the time.
  - ✓ Use an external monitor that allows you to spread your work out on a bigger screen.
  - ✓ Wear blue light glasses if you will spend significant time at a computer screen.
  - ✓ Use over-the-ear headphones to focus on the audio during meetings or to listen to focus music when you are heads down on a project.
- ▷ Set good office boundaries.
  - ✓ Check in and out of work with rituals that help you separate and transition between your professional and personal life.
  - ✓ Take breaks by putting them in your schedule and truly honoring them.
  - ✓ Close your office door as a sign to your family that you are busy working and should not be interrupted.
- ▷ Apply best practices to your work effort.
  - ✓ Set weekly intentions on Monday for what you want to have accomplished by Friday. Focus on no more than three things that allow you to move important projects forward, not a big list that can't be achieved.

- ✓ Keep your workspace organized and your objectives and key files easily accessible.

- ✓ Proactively communicate with colleagues, staying focused on essential, clear messages. Create virtual opportunities for watercooler chats and personal connections.

▷ Manage your career.

- ✓ Keep a running document with your accomplishments, challenges, and professional development goals so you have a written record for each position. Before meeting with your supervisor for work evaluations, review this list so you have a good set of talking points going into the conversation. Also use these notes to update your resume or inform your next job search.

- ✓ As opportunities grow, remote work positions will remain competitive. Continue to look for ways to enhance your skills, find mentors, and take on bigger projects.

- ✓ Continue networking and forming genuine relationships in your industry.

- ✓ Always be prepared for a promotion or your next great career opportunity.

Remote work is the way of the future. It works for many employees and many companies, and technology will only get better and faster to accommodate the needs of remote workers and employers. Military spouses are uniquely positioned to benefit from and thrive in remote work roles when they know how to find, get, and navigate them.

As you go forward, keep in mind all the things you learned about yourself and your ideal position, company culture, and relationships with coworkers. In a remote environment, leaning into what you do well and what will best serve you and the company sets you up for greater success and growth along the way. While it might take time, there are plenty of employers where your perspective and experience as a person and a military spouse will be welcomed.

Your remote job hunt might begin because you are a military spouse, but your remote career will thrive because of your proactive efforts to make the most of this journey!

Afterword

As I type this, I've just completed my ninth (and hopefully final) move for my husband's military career. During the past decade as a remote worker, I have been able to push myself as an entrepreneur, work as an employee, start a nonprofit, and do so many other things thanks to the ability to connect with others online. When I wrote this book, I wanted to provide a resource guide with strategies and suggestions for other military spouses to be able to do the same, no matter what their intended remote career looks like.

You have taken the first step toward success in your remote journey: educating yourself. Though this book covers many topics relevant to your remote work journey, the remote work world will continue to evolve. Whether you are early in your career or more established, it is your responsibility to keep your skillset and resume updated along with it. Now that you know how to position yourself for remote work, find the right opportunities, network and build connections with movers and shakers, go through the application process with confidence, and excel in your remote work position, the sky is the limit.

Being a military spouse in a remote work world is a strength. You are accustomed to maintaining important relationships between great physical distances; you can handle a lot of change; and you have already mastered the resilience it takes to push past obstacles in your career path. By building a work life you love, you can support your spouse's career and still have meaningful employment that drives you and contributes to your family's income. Finding the right fit in terms of role, company culture, pay, and flexibility is both possible and probable when you use the strategies you've learned in this book. Now, go get to work!

Acknowledgments

I owe a great deal of gratitude to many members of the military community, particularly other military and veteran spouses. Many of them have helped me navigate my own remote career and have served as valuable thought leaders and colleagues as I worked on this book. I'm especially grateful for the support I've received from Kimber Hill, Jaime Chapman, and Jay Sheehan. I also owe a thank you to Kelly Grivner-Kelly, who graciously allowed me to interview her about remote work experiences for spouses.

To my business manager, Melissa Swire, your support and friendship mean the world, and I wouldn't be able to do all that I am without you. You inspire me daily.

Thank you also to Upwork for your support of my non-profit, Operation Freelance, where we give military spouses free online entrepreneurship training.

Finally, to the team at Elva Resa Publishing, thank you for sharing the vision that military spouse careers matter and for helping shape this book and its message accordingly.

9 781934 617656